BEGINNER'S GUIDE TO
ECHOLOCATION
FOR THE BLIND
AND VISUALLY IMPAIRED

BEGINNER'S GUIDE TO ECHOLOCATION

BEGINNER'S GUIDE TO ECHOLOCATION FOR THE BLIND AND VISUALLY IMPAIRED

LEARNING TO SEE
WITH YOUR EARS

BY: TIM JOHNSON
CO-AUTHORED BY:
JUSTIN LOUCHART

BEGINNER'S GUIDE TO ECHOLOCATION

Copyright © 2012 Tim Johnson. All rights reserved. No part of this publication may be re-produced (except for reviews), stored in a retrieval system, or transmitted in any form by any means, electronic, mechanical, photocopying, recording or otherwise, without the written prior permission of the author.

PLEASE NOTE: The creators and publishers of this book disclaim any liabilities or loss in connection with following any of the practices, exercises, and advice contained herein. To reduce the risk of injury or any other harm, the reader should consult a professional orientation and mobility specialist for proper guidance. The instructions and advice supplied in this book are not in any way intended as a substitute for medical, mental, or emotional counseling with a licensed physician or healthcare provider.

Although the views and opinions of World Access for the Blind are not directly reflected in this book, the procedures, strategies, and instructional materials are a direct result of our cooperation and philosophical agreement.
ISBN-10: **1480153516**
ISBN-13: **978-1480153516**

First Edition

Author's Blog: http://learnecholocation.blogspot.com

DEDICATION

TO ALL THOSE WITH
A PASSION FOR LIVING.

BEGINNER'S GUIDE TO ECHOLOCATION

BEGINNER'S GUIDE TO ECHOLOCATION

TABLE OF CONTENTS

- Preface
- Part 1 – Introduction to Echolocation
    - What is Echolocation?
    - The Profound Benefits of Echolocation
    - Overcoming Vision Loss
    - Why Isn't Echolocation More Commonly Used?
    - James Holman – Blind Adventurer
    - Can Fully-sighted People Learn Echolocation?
    - Why Learn Echolocation as a Sighted Person?
    - The Use of Echolocation in Submarines
- Part 2 – Beginning Your Journey
    - Overcoming the Challenge of Learning Echolocation
    - Shifting Your Sensory Paradigm
    - Keeping an Open Mind
    - Make Calculated Mistakes!
- Part 3 – Start Experiencing Echolocation
    - What is a Sound Wave?
    - Understanding the Qualities of Sound
    - The Basics of an Echo

BEGINNER'S GUIDE TO ECHOLOCATION

- Getting in Tune With Your Sense of Sound
- Sensitizing Your Hearing Using Music
- The Sensation of Echolocation
- Experience Echolocation While Riding In a Car
- Echolocation Awareness Exercise
- Echolocation in Terms of Reverb
- Part 4 – Signals
  - Passive Versus Active Echolocation
  - Passive Echolocation Signals
  - Properties of a Good Click Signal
  - Various Clicking Techniques
  - The Science of a Signal
  - Why a 3kHz Signal is Optimal for Echolocation
  - Clicking Devices and Alternatives
  - Finding *Your* Signal
- Part 5 – Echolocation Lessons
  - Seeing Something Versus Nothing
  - Right Versus Left
  - Above Versus Below
  - Learning to Gauge Distance
  - Calibrating to Angled Surfaces
  - Calibrating to Round Surfaces
  - Learning to Distinguish Materials

BEGINNER'S GUIDE TO ECHOLOCATION

- o Frequency Absorption Characteristics of a Variety of Materials
- o Making the Sensation Your Own
- o Locating a Doorway
- o Navigating a Familiar Environment
- o Walking a Familiar Path
- o Using the Visual Cortex to Build Non-visual Imagery
- Part 6 – Continuing Education and Training
  - o How Can I Become An Expert?
  - o Where Do I Go From Here?
  - o More Resources

BEGINNER'S GUIDE TO ECHOLOCATION

"THE WORLD IS FULL OF MAGICAL THINGS, PATIENTLY WAITING FOR OUR SENSES TO GROW SHARPER."

WILLIAM BUTLER YEATS

BEGINNER'S GUIDE TO ECHOLOCATION

PREFACE

In order to get the most out of life, I strongly hold that we must experience everything first hand and perform all things we do to the very best of our ability. Echolocation is a skill that can be learned by anyone to help gain a new perspective and thereby a new way of experiencing the world. Through my own experience and research, I am convinced that using echolocation is an excellent way for any person who is partially sighted or completely blind to have the benefit of understanding their surroundings and being able to gain the independence and self-confidence required to truly experience the world in ways they might never have imagined possible.

This book is an introduction to the concepts of echolocation. It is not a complete and comprehensive guide nor is it the recommended method for learning echolocation to a high proficiency. In order to become proficient, it is always recommended that you find a mentor or teacher to guide you through the complex process of learning this unique skill. However, if you are unable, or not ready, to commit to one-on-one intensive training, let this book be a tool to help you begin your journey and discover the power of echolocation and the impact it can have on your mobility, leading to a richer, more fulfilling life.

This book will provide you with a fundamental understanding of sound and echoes (what they are and how they work), how echolocation is used now, and how it can be practiced and refined by anyone willing to learn. It will also teach you what will be required in order to take on this unique and profound challenge. It will give you real examples of echolocation techniques you might already use and offer techniques for experiencing echolocation even if you don't know where to start or what echolocation is.

Finally, it will provide a regimen of lessons to use on your own to begin experiencing, understanding, and honing this skill and improving it to the level that suits your requirements. These lessons have been designed to take you step by step from the very beginning and improve your skills far beyond that of the average person.

It is a privilege for me to publish this book and contribute this information to those people who want more fulfillment in their lives. Whether you are completely blind, partially sighted, or fully sighted, the goal of this book is to:

BEGINNER'S GUIDE TO ECHOLOCATION

- Raise your awareness of your own body and mind.
- Raise your awareness of your immediate environment.
- Raise public awareness for echolocation as a tool for people who are visually impaired.
- Open your eyes to underutilized capabilities of human kind.

BEGINNER'S GUIDE TO ECHOLOCATION

BEGINNER'S GUIDE TO ECHOLOCATION

PART 1

INTRODUCTION TO ECHOLOCATION

WHAT IS ECHOLOCATION?

Echolocation is the method of interpreting the sounds created by echoes from surrounding objects in order to determine where the objects are in relation to you. It's not magic nor does it require special abilities or even years of training. Humans can learn to interpret echoes and sound reverberations to *see* the world around them with surprisingly little training. Objects from very large to very small can be detected, and this technique can be used to orient one's self and navigate through complex and foreign environments. At times, much more information about the surrounding environment can be gathered using echolocation than vision itself, such as texture and the material of objects.

Dolphins, bats, and whales use a form of echolocation as well as many other species, but their frequencies are generally far higher than what humans can detect. Sound is a wave of energy in the form of pressure that is emitted from a source and travels outward from the source until it fades away or comes in contact with an object. If it comes in contact with a hard object, it bounces off and reflects some properties of the object in the way that it bounces. Many people who are blind utilize this tactic via listening to the reverberations of their own footsteps, tapping their cane, or by making a clicking sound with their mouth.

Echolocation is the learned ability to sense the size, shape, location, distance, and even construct of objects surrounding you without touching them (with your hands, cane, or otherwise) or being told about them. As a hearing person, you have this capability in the same way that you have the capability to enjoy good music.

If you've been without vision for more than a couple of years, you probably use it to some extent without even knowing it. Most blind people, in their effort to figure out what's going on around them, know this concept, but are unsure what to call it. Some refer to it as *facial pressure*, *air currents*, or *ambient sound*. Before learning about echolocation, you might think this is a primitive way of getting a *sense* of the size of a room, or the location of a door, etc.

Most people don't know that this is a skill that can be learned and improved upon in order to eventually give them a very real *vision* of the world and the obstacles around them to an ever-increasing level of detail. Some completely blind people have been known to use echolocation to be able to *see* well enough to distinguish the difference between two small objects on a table, find a ball in an open field, determine the level of liquid in a cup, and even go mountain biking!

Senior scientist Dr. Mel Goodale, from the University of Western Ontario, said:

> "It is clear that echolocation enables blind people to do things that are otherwise thought to be impossible without vision, and in this way it can provide blind and vision-impaired people with a high degree of independence in their daily lives."

THE PROFOUND BENEFITS OF ECHOLOCATION

Echolocation is a physical ability that we possess naturally and has been proven effective by blind people all over the world. Scientists have performed extensive research on this subject, but sadly, it is not used by most blind people. In fact, many people have never heard of it.

Compared to other animal species, human beings have very limited physical capabilities and are, in large part, quite fragile and unprotected from the elements of nature. Hundreds of thousands of years of human evolution are to be attributed to the fact that we use brainpower, tools, and the minimal physical abilities that we do have, and we must use these things in the most effective way we possibly can. Echolocation is an ability that has gone unacknowledged for many thousands of these years. Certainly, there have been people who use it, most likely blind (the case of James Holman stands out as notable and inspirational amongst many blind people who claimed to be able to see objects via *pressure* on their face, or *facial pressure*), but it has not been brought to the attention of the mainstream public until quite recently.

BEGINNER'S GUIDE TO ECHOLOCATION

If your parents had told you that you could hear the sound reflected off of objects and asked you, "Where does the tree sound like it is?" just like they asked you "What does the tree feel like?" then you probably would have grown up with at least an acknowledgment of the existence of this ability.

It is human nature for people to explore their own abilities. Therefore, you probably would have practiced or at least noticed this sense in your development. Now, what if people had been developing this ability for the past 10,000 years, just like the abilities of speech, walking or running; imagine where we would be. The world of darkness and blindness would be so much less foreign to us and there would be many opportunities and abilities which inherently implement echolocation that would easily become apparent should we refine this ability.

We have so much room for development in the area of echolocation and so much to learn. We have not reached the final plateau in learning about ourselves. In fact, that would be an outright impossibility. Each new characteristic or trait we adopt becomes a part of who we are, and it defines the next goal and the next milestone for our society and our race. Each step we take to improve and better adapt to our circumstances is one more step in the never-ending path of the evolution of our species. For tens of thousands of years, we have been adapting and overcoming adverse circumstances. This is what makes us stronger. This is what makes us human.

"IT IS ENTIRELY POSSIBLE THAT BEHIND THE PERCEPTION OF OUR SENSES, WORLDS ARE HIDDEN OF WHICH WE ARE UNAWARE."

ALBERT EINSTEIN

OVERCOMING VISION LOSS WITH ECHOLOCATION

Millions of people around the world live with blindness every day. In June 2012, the World Health Organization estimated that 39 million people are blind and an additional 246 million have low vision. If you are struggling with vision loss, or if you have been blind from a young age, you know all about the obstacles that make independence difficult in your daily life. Many countries are fortunate to have modern technologies and complex methods of overcoming these adversities, such as schools and foundations for the blind, guide dogs, and even the simple collapsible cane that is not available in many less fortunate countries. However, the World Health Organization also estimates that 90% of all visually impaired persons live in developing countries.

If you do not have the conveniences or support structure to assist you in overcoming these obstacles, you may feel isolated and completely dependent upon family members to care for you. I know that there are hundreds of thousands of blind people in less-fortunate places in the world who have no one to care for them, and they lead extremely solitary, unfulfilled, and unhealthy lives. Whether you are blessed with modern conveniences and support to help overcome your challenges or not, echolocation is a concept you should come to understand.

With open-mindedness and diligent practice, anyone can learn this skill and use it to help them live a more fulfilling, active, and healthier life.

BEGINNER'S GUIDE TO ECHOLOCATION

"THE WISE DON'T EXPECT TO FIND LIFE WORTH LIVING; THEY MAKE IT THAT WAY."

ANONYMOUS

WHY ISN'T ECHOLOCATION MORE COMMONLY USED?

The three main reasons people shy away from learning echolocation are because:

1. THEY HAVE NEVER HEARD OF IT

With this book and the increasing awareness of echolocation, thanks to the work done by World Access for the Blind and other organizations teaching new methods of blind mobility and the increasingly large body of knowledge available worldwide, it is sure to gain momentum in the media and especially within the blind community. In this era of our society, when something like this offers great value, it will rapidly surface and become evident that this is the next logical addition to blind mobility instruction.

2. THEY DO NOT UNDERSTAND IT

There is so much to life that we don't understand. Even the most advanced scientists in the world cannot explain exactly how the brain works. It's up to each one of us as individuals to explore and discover our own capabilities and limitations. Once we have discovered and understand our limitations, only then will we be able to break free of them using creative thinking and diligent training. As we will discuss later in this book, open-mindedness and a willingness to try new things can help shift our understanding in incredible ways.

3. THEY BELIEVE IT IS AN INSURMOUNTABLE CHALLENGE

The skill of echolocation is nothing short of astounding. Unbelievable is a word commonly used to describe it, which unfortunately creates a stigma that it is insurmountable for most people. Nothing is insurmountable. If one person on this planet can achieve something, that means anyone else can do it if they set their mind to it. How to get there is the tricky part, but it's also the fun part.

We should use information provided by science. It's sometimes misguided, sometimes misused, but in essence and in definition, science speaks the truth and is an incredible learning tool. But, science alone will not be a solution for all problems; there are things that it simply does not encompass, or has yet to explain. To learn an internal skill like echolocation, you will also need to employ introspection.

> *INTROSPECTION is the self-examination of one's conscious thoughts and feelings. In psychology, the process of introspection relies exclusively on the purposeful and rational self-observation of one's mental state; however, introspection is sometimes referenced in a spiritual context as the examination of one's soul. Introspection is closely related to the philosophical concept of human self-reflection, and is contrasted with external observation.*
>
> *Wikipedia*

This means looking into yourself and finding answers, solutions, and techniques that work for you. It is taking what you know and piecing the puzzle together. It is creating new and unique knowledge from nothing. Anyone can do it, and everyone should do it.

Once you understand the proven truths of a matter and have accepted the science as fact, and once you have opened your mind to the possibility that this skill is something you can achieve in your own unique way, you're on the right path. You will be able to learn this ability using simple methods and exercises and by implementing principles proven by science. You will quickly be able to shape the skill into something completely unique to your own mind and circumstances in a way that only you will truly understand.

"ALL TRUTHS ARE EASY TO UNDERSTAND ONCE THEY ARE DISCOVERED; THE POINT IS TO DISCOVER THEM."

GALILEO GALILEI

JAMES HOLMAN: BLIND ADVENTURER

James Holman (15 October 1786 – 29 July 1857), fellow of the Royal Society, and known as the *Blind Traveler*, was a British adventurer, author, and social observer, best known for his extensive travelling and the writings he compiled to document them. In addition to being completely blind, he also had limited mobility due to debilitating pain. Despite his adversities, he undertook a series of solo journeys that were unprecedented both in their scope and the fact that he undertook them using echolocation. In 1866, journalist William Jerdan wrote that:

"From Marco Polo to Mungo Park, no three of the most famous travelers, grouped together, would exceed the extent and variety of countries traversed by our blind countryman."

Holman was born the son of an apothecary in Exeter and entered into the British Royal Navy in 1798. He was appointed lieutenant in April 1807, and in 1810 while on the Guerriere off the coast of the Americas, he was struck with an illness that first affected his joints and eventually his vision. At the age of 25, he was rendered completely blind.

In recognition of the fact that his affliction was related to his military duty, he was appointed to the Naval Knights of Windsor in 1812 with a lifetime grant of care in Windsor Castle provided that he attend church service twice daily in return for room and board. The quietness of such a life, however, did not harmonize with his active habits and keen interests making him physically ill. He requested multiple leaves of absence on health grounds, first to study medicine and literature at the University of Edinburgh, then to go abroad on a Grand Tour from 1819 to 1821 when he journeyed through France, Italy, Switzerland, parts of Germany bordering on the Rhine, Belgium, and the Netherlands. Upon his return, he published *The Narrative of a Journey through France, etc.* (London, 1822).

He again set out in 1822 with the incredible intention of making a trip around the world from west to east, something which, at the time, was almost unheard of by a lone traveler, blind or not. He travelled through Russia as far east as the Mongolian frontier of Irkutsk. At this point, he was suspected by the Czar of being a spy who might publicize the extensive activities of the Russian-

American Company should he travel further east and was forcibly conducted back to the frontiers of Poland. He returned home via Austria, Saxony, Prussia, and Hanover. He then published *Travels through Russia, Siberia, etc.* (London, 1825).

Shortly afterwards he set out again to accomplish by somewhat different means the trip which had been cut short by the Russian authorities. An account of his remarkable achievement was published in four volumes in 1834-1835, under the title of *A Voyage Round the World, including Travels in Africa, Asia, Australasia, America, etc., from 1827 to 1832.*

Holman was elected as a Fellow of the Royal Society (UK) and of the Linnaean Society (UK). Charles Darwin, in *The Voyage of the Beagle*, cited Holman's writings as a source on the flora of the Indian Ocean. On Fernando Po Island, now part of Equatorial Guinea, the British Government named the Holman River in his honor, commemorating his contributions to fighting the slave trade in the region during the 1820s.

His last journeys were through Spain, Portugal, Moldavia, Montenegro, Syria, and Turkey. Within a week after finishing an autobiography, *Holman's Narratives of His Travels*, he died in London on 29 July

1857. His last work was never published and has likely not survived.

While his early works were generally well received (only partially as a novelty), over time competitors and skeptics introduced doubt into the public consciousness about the reliability of Holman's *observations*. In a time when blind people were thought to be totally helpless and usually given a bowl to beg with, Holman's ability to sense his surroundings by the reverberations of a tapped cane or horse's hoof-beats was unfathomable.

The Wikisource 1911 Encyclopedia Project

There is no doubt that James Holman paved the way for people to start considering the possibility and benefits that this foreign skill could have for others. Likely, they did not express this consideration publicly in order to avoid mockery and ridicule, but his story continues to inspire people around the world today in a time when open-mindedness and acceptance of new ways of thinking are celebrated and encouraged.

CAN FULLY SIGHTED PEOPLE LEARN ECHOLOCATION?

It is commonly understood that echolocation is easier for the blind practitioner to learn. The word *easy* is a relative term and the ease of learning any skill will be different for everyone. There are many clear advantages that blind people do have over sighted people when learning echolocation. Firstly, the visual cortex of the brain, being unutilized, or under-utilized, is capable of being reallocated for other tasks and abilities such as reading Braille, having heightened hearing sensitivity, and performing echolocation.

Secondly, and very importantly, blind people have the built-in commitment mechanism of being required to use some form of orientation other than vision. They can implement the skills of echolocation into their daily life and immediately realize the benefits it can have. Every skill learned is forward progress while a sighted person must designate times to train blindfolded or with closed eyes, at which point they may become very uncomfortable and unsure of themselves. These training times will likely be less than 5% of the time that a blind person would spend becoming familiar with the same principles.

However, there is no reason sighted people cannot learn echolocation. I have met many sighted people with a desire to learn this skill due to a mere fascination of the capabilities of the human mind and body. Of course, it will require diligent practice and it will likely take much longer to learn and become comfortable with echolocation than it will for a blind counterpart, and there is the threat that failing to practice for a given amount of time will result in diminishing skill level.

I, of course, would highly recommend that anyone learn to use, or at least understand, echolocation, regardless of your current level of vision, whether to increase your confidence in moving about the world or to glean insight into the dormant capabilities of your own senses. The realization of the amount of awareness that echolocation provides is an astounding and magnificent experience that should be shared by all.

WHY LEARN ECHOLOCATION AS A SIGHTED PERSON?

The benefits of acquiring the skill of echolocation as a blind person have an obvious impact on the way you interact with your surroundings on a daily basis. Any insight that echolocation can offer adds directly to one's ability to perceive their environment.

As a sighted person, to train in echolocation, you must close your eyes. This is inherently reducing your amount of perception and starting at a level that you are not comfortable with and you may have very low confidence navigating in the dark. So, why would you want to learn?

I asked sighted people in a survey why they wanted to learn echolocation and below are some of the common responses:

- To continually and aggressively exercise my brain.
- To be able to navigate in the dark better.
- To develop my understanding of visually impaired colleagues and co-workers.

- The human mind and body is a fascinating subject, and it's amazing that echolocation is a skill we can all learn.
- To be able to continue my life normally if I ever were to lose my sight.

It's wonderful to see so many people interested in developing themselves in new and unique ways. As the author of this book, I feel lucky to be able to work with and learn from so many interesting people, including you!

A UNIQUE LEARNING OPPORTUNITY

In today's world, people are becoming more and more open to exploring new methods of learning and growing as a society. My echolocation blog is a good example of that. I can put this very obscure information out there on the web and there are hundreds even thousands of people who read it and respond to me with their feedback and stories about how they are learning echolocation. It's wonderful to speak with so many people opening their minds to new possibilities and seeking out new challenges. Seeking new challenges is truly a great frontier unto itself.

Working the brain muscle is always a good thing to do. Things like learning new languages, learning a musical instrument, learning to cook, learning how to juggle or otherwise improving your coordination is great medicine for the brain. Notice how each of these examples starts with the word *learning*? Do you see a pattern? Learning echolocation is, of course, a great brain exercise, but the fact that echolocation is likely to be a completely foreign concept requires entirely new channels to be opened in the mind.

Eventually – not this decade and probably not this century – but eventually, I'm certain that echolocation will become a mainstream mode of perception for all humans, blind and sighted. It will be taught from childhood and will have several applications in daily life. It can help us become a better race and a better society. This is the natural way of evolution and new skills like this have been added to the human skill set for thousands of years. We will always continue to grow and develop as a species. We can position ourselves ahead of the curve and essentially see into the future by recognizing these skills now and being part of the driving force that helps them propagate to future generations.

Every day we should challenge ourselves. This is the only way to improve ourselves. Each day that passes without overcoming adversity, or learning something

BEGINNER'S GUIDE TO ECHOLOCATION

new, or standing up to face a new challenge is a precious day wasted. A phrase that we would recite in Portuguese at the beginning of a martial arts class I attended was "Each day that passes, I am improving everything that I do." Every day I want to become a better person and challenge myself in ways that I did not challenge myself the day before. Echolocation is a great new horizon on which I find many challenges, and it is for that reason that I find it so alluring.

THE USE OF ECHOLOCATION IN SUBMARINES

The best-known application of echolocation in humans is in the field of submarine navigation. Submarine sonar technicians are basically blind. The water pressure at these depths makes it impossible to install windows on the outside of the submarine leaving them with only their sense of sound to detect objects. Since the 1940s, submarines have used the echo of strong pulses of sound to determine where the ocean floor is and identify other obstacles like reefs, islands, continental formations, or whales. The returning sounds are relayed via headphones to a specially trained technician whose job it is to interpret these sounds and to guide the submarine and its crew safely through complete darkness.

BEGINNER'S GUIDE TO ECHOLOCATION

PART 2

BEGINNING YOUR JOURNEY

IS ECHOLOCATION FOR ME?

OVERCOMING THE CHALLENGE OF LEARNING ECHOLOCATION

Anyone looking to learn anything will always have challenges. The process of learning requires an expenditure of energy that you will never get back. That is to say, each moment in life is different and unique and we are given the opportunity to use these moments however we like, and it is how we use these moments that make us unique, powerful, strong, and independent. For each moment of your life that you spend diligently learning a skill, you will get something far more valuable for your time and effort after taking on that challenge, oftentimes far more than you sought to learn in the first place.

Life as a whole is a challenge. It is an expenditure of energy to reach a goal. Know your goals. Embrace the challenge, and make the journey your own. Perhaps most importantly, enjoy the learning process.

SHIFTING YOUR SENSORY PARADIGM

Everyone knows about the five senses. We're taught at a very young age to understand these five basic input methods and to utilize them the best we can in our daily life in order to best understand the world around us:

- Sight
- Sound
- Smell
- Taste
- Touch

However, sometimes what we learn in school can be limiting, especially things that we learn at a very young age and, for the remainder of our lives, believe to be true. These five senses become one of our paradigms. We know that the five senses must be everything; that's what the teacher says. When I was little, I was also taught that there were **nine** planets . . . that has been the topic of several astronomical discussions over the past 10 years or so, and it is clearly an issue of the actual definition of the word planet. No one wants to add more planets to the line-up because there's only supposed to be nine!

BEGINNER'S GUIDE TO ECHOLOCATION

Radically changing your belief or theory on a certain subject is the definition of a *paradigm shift*. It's a social, sometimes psychological, struggle to shift one's paradigm from believing one thing to believing something different. Once a belief or a fundamental understanding of something is ingrained into our minds, it can be **very** difficult to change that belief or shift that paradigm.

Shifting your paradigm is something that can be practiced in and of itself by doing things like:

- Feeding yourself with the opposite hand.
- Putting your pants on opposite leg first.
- Getting out of your comfort zone by trying something you never thought you would.
- Practicing mindfulness meditation.

I believe that there are more than five senses. Again, this debate will lie in the definition of the word *sense* and whether or not each *sense* has a dedicated organ. But to me, a sense can be related to a *channel* for information input, not necessarily an organ.

BEGINNER'S GUIDE TO ECHOLOCATION

Some other senses that have been explored by science are:

- Echolocation
- Proprioception
- Interoception
- Equilibrioception
- Thermal Perception
- Duration or Time Perception
- Magnetoreception
- Extra Sensory Perception (ESP or Intuition)

Echolocation – As far as organs go, this sense uses primarily the ears, but it is completely different from the sense of hearing because there is a drastically different set of data that can be obtained when one is familiar with and comfortable with using this channel of their perception.

Proprioception – This is the sense of the physical positioning of one's own body: joints, limbs, orientation, etc. This is discussed in-depth in martial arts, dance, and many other sports. If you move your arms around without looking at them, you have a sense of where they are. Some people have been known to lose this sense due to brain injury or other trauma, and it is completely debilitating.

Interoception – This is our sense of the internal well-being of our bodies. It's how we sense our stress levels, our mood, disposition, etc. While it does not necessarily relate to an external stimulus, it is certainly something that must be considered a channel of perception.

Equilibrioception – Our sense of balance, called equilibrioception, makes use of our eyes, ears, and sense of proprioception, above. The vestibular system of the inner ear also plays an important role in this sensation as the movement of fluids in the inner ear help tell the brain which way the head is turning and which way the body as a whole is moving.

Thermal Perception – This is the ability to sense changes in temperature. It could be interpreted that this is part of the sense of "touch" but I would argue that it's a slightly different channel, or different implementation of this sense.

Duration or Time Perception – This is the channel through which we sense the duration of events in time. This cannot be directly perceived but rather reconstructed by certain channels in the brain.

Magnetoreception – This is the ability to detect the direction one is facing (latitude, longitude, and altitude) based on the Earth's magnetic field. Directional awareness is most commonly observed in birds, though it is also thought to be present to a limited extent in humans. It is hypothesized that this sense is what makes it possible for birds to migrate thousands of miles and often end up in the exact same spot. Tests have been done to prove that even a sedated bird can easily find its way home after being moved a long distance.

ESP (Intuition) – A sense that may be controversial and experienced differently by different people, this is a channel of reception in the brain whereby people acquire information not through any organ but directly by the brain from external sources. Telepathy, clairvoyance, precognition, psychic ability, or intuition are other words used for this sense.

These are just a few simple examples of senses that we don't often think about, but that may have great impact on our daily lives whether we know it or not. I think it would be best to teach children about the *senses* as opposed to the *five senses*. This would eliminate the psychological limitations and allow children to learn of the entirety of their senses. If a new sense is discovered, or developed, it would be in our best interest as a species to teach and further develop that sense.

KEEPING AN OPEN MIND

Echolocation is a unique skill that will reward you with an entirely new way of *seeing* the world, but it will require completely new and different ways of thinking. Imagine if prehistoric man had not thought outside the box and never decided to take a perfectly good piece of food and put it over a fire – a fire that was known for destroying everything it came in contact with. At first glance, that wouldn't be a great idea, and it would be a waste of a long day of hunting or gathering. Fortunately, it turned out to be common practice for helping to tenderize and breakdown our foods to make them easier to digest.

Opposing convention and taking the path less travelled is the spirit of innovation. It is what has motivated the human race to become increasingly intelligent and prosperous. None of the great minds in human history allowed themselves to be limited by convention or prior schools of thought. If you approach this learning process with preconceived notions, you have already limited your capacity to prosper. Remember that knowledge can be garnered from unsuspecting sources and that all new information and experiences should be thoroughly considered before being implemented or discarded. As with anything new, remember that even the sky cannot limit what you can achieve.

BEGINNER'S GUIDE TO ECHOLOCATION

"THE ULTIMATE AUTHORITY MUST ALWAYS REST WITH THE INDIVIDUAL'S OWN REASON AND CRITICAL ANALYSIS."

THE DALAI LAMA

MAKE CALCULATED MISTAKES!

One of the most important aspects of learning new skills that most people neglect is the power and beauty of the mistake. When a mistake occurs, there is a profound moment of pure learning that you will not find anywhere else. I'm not saying take a running start for the stairwell here; *calculated* mistakes are the best. Make mistakes in a place where you can estimate the severity of the outcome of the mistakes and where you have an exit strategy in order to maintain your personal safety.

For instance, during echolocation training protect your toes, and do not practice barefoot. Objects near your feet can be hard to perceive, so wear shoes that allow you to kick things like curbstones and end tables without being injured. Go slowly at first. There may be low hanging branches, shelving, or open cupboard doors that you may run into. The best way to stay safe at first is to take it slow. There is no reason to rush when training. Another method would be to have a sighted guide act as a spotter, not to give you hints, but simply to notify you of possible dangers.

BEGINNER'S GUIDE TO ECHOLOCATION

Once you have addressed your personal safety and feel that you understand the severity of the potential hazards around you, it's time to make mistakes.

In order to improve your current physical and mental limitations, you will need to push your limits, or leave your *comfort zone*. Doing things that you are not *quite* comfortable with, will help you gain the confidence to succeed. Your physical and mental limitations are generally governed by your level of self-confidence. In order to eventually exceed those limits, you will essentially need to be *slightly* over-confident and fail. The idea here is to make them small failures and learn from them. By being only slightly over-confident, the failures and mistakes will be less threatening and non-injurious, thus allowing you to learn. This will allow you to first, understand the limitations, and then figure out how to exceed them. Determine the little things, the details that you can adjust or focus on in order to improve your ability to echolocate.

For instance, say that during your first echolocation training exercises that require you to walk, you notice that you are only shuffling very slowly and identifying obstacles with reasonable success, I would recommend that once you are comfortable at a certain level, you slowly start to pick up the pace and push yourself just outside of your comfort zone. Once you are out of your comfort zone again, you should be making mistakes, but only minor mistakes that you understand and can rectify. This will ensure that you are always learning and not reaching a plateau.

Now that you are ready to make mistakes, you are ready to begin experiencing echolocation.

I will add to this that it is generally encouraged that blind practitioners continue to use their cane during echolocation when travelling in unfamiliar environments for safety reasons.

BEGINNER'S GUIDE TO ECHOLOCATION

"DO NOT FEAR MISTAKES.
YOU WILL KNOW FAILURE.
CONTINUE TO REACH OUT."

BENJAMIN FRANKLIN

PART 3

START EXPERIENCING ECHOLOCATION

UNDERSTANDING SOUNDS AND "TUNING IN"

WHAT IS A SOUND WAVE?

A sound wave is a mechanical pressure wave that is created by any vibrating object in a medium like air or water. In order for human ears to hear the sound, the vibration must be within about 20 – 20,000 Hertz (or vibrations per second). This defines the spectrum of audible sound. 20 Hertz is a very low-pitched sound and 20,000 Hertz is a very high-pitched sound.

If you move your hand back and forth in a pool of water, it will create ripples on the surface of the water. The peaks of the ripples rise above the surface of the water, while the low points dip below the normal surface of the water. This is the same as the concept of a sound wave through air, except that sound waves in air propagate outward from the sound source in all three directions (not just two, as on the surface of the water). Air molecules compress together and then relax apart just like the ripples on the water. The compressed molecules represent the ripple peaks where the air pressure has been increased to above normal atmospheric pressure, and between the peaks, the pressure is negative and has dipped below atmospheric pressure.

As sound waves (or water ripples) move away from the source, the peaks and valleys get less pronounced, and hence the strength of the wave fades, and the sound gets quieter.

The volume or strength of sound is measured using Sound Pressure Level or SPL. This is the difference between the pressure of the surrounding air, and the sum of the pressure in the sound wave. There is no quantifiable method of measuring sound; this method MUST involve a relative comparison between two sounds, or two pressure levels.

A steady vibration or oscillation will provide only a simple, steady tone. It is the other characteristics of sound that we will discuss in the following section that help us to interpret the sound as music, speech, or other things.

UNDERSTANDING THE QUALITIES OF SOUND

Here are a few concepts and words that may be used throughout this book. In coming to understand how to use the subtleties of sound for something as difficult as echolocating, it is important to attempt to gain as complete an understanding as possible about all facets and attributes of sound.

PITCH

Pitch is the perception of a high or low sound. This is similar to the frequency of a sound; however, while frequency puts a value on the number of times the sound pressure in the air oscillates each second, pitch is the more subjective comparison of different sounds with respect to one another. Humans are said to be able to identify the differences between 1,400 different pitches along the spectrum of audible sound.

LOUDNESS

Also called amplitude, volume, or sound level, this is the intensity of a sound. This quality is measured in relative comparisons to other sounds, or a baseline sound level defined as zero decibels.

PHASE

Phase is the increase and decrease in pressure in any single vibration. As sound waves overlap and crisscross in three-dimensional space, they create different shapes the same way ripples on water from two pebbles come together to create a blended version of the two wave patterns. As the high-pressure portions of waves overlap, they form an even higher-pressure peak, and conversely, a lower-pressure peak for overlapping low-pressure portions. This can cause two steady tones to combine to create a new tone with a fluctuating or pulsating quality to it.

DIRECTION

Hearing with two ears allows us to distinguish left/right, high/low and front/back directionality. If a sound is heard by one ear and then the other, the brain will automatically process that information and tell you that the sound came from the side of the ear to first register the sound. Similarly, the shape of our ear cavities provides us with the subtle information about whether a sound is high or low, and back or front.

DISTANCE

BEGINNER'S GUIDE TO ECHOLOCATION

Distance is the perception of how near or far away a sound's source is. This is perceived in part due to having two ears and being able to sense directionality, and in part due to recognizing the effect of reverb, echo, and other variations in tone or timbre due to how far away the sound is and the various paths it travels to reach one's ears.

TIMBRE

Also referred to as tone color, this is the perceived quality of any sound's multiple frequencies as they change over time. This quality gives us the capacity to differentiate between, for instance, a violin and a trumpet. It has to do with the fluctuations in signal over time. Higher frequency signals blend with lower frequencies to create a unique sound wave, thus a unique sound. Any sound that lasts for less than 4ms is said to be an indistinguishable click.

THE BASICS OF AN ECHO

THE WORD ECHO DERIVES FROM THE GREEK ἦχος (ĒCHOS), MEANING *SOUND*.

An echo is a reflection of sound off an object, arriving at the listener sometime after the initial sound is created. Typical examples are the echoes created by a large building, a canyon, or by the walls of an enclosed room. A true echo is a single reflection of the sound source. As a sound emanates from its source, sound waves travel radially outward from it in all directions through space. As they encounter an object or a change in the medium through which they are travelling, they are interrupted and reflected back depending on the surface texture and construct of the object.

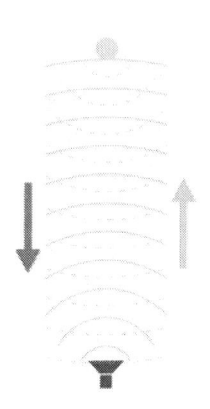

GETTING IN TUNE WITH YOUR SENSE OF SOUND

Getting in tune with your senses, or becoming more aware of yourself and your surroundings will be important when learning echolocation as it relies heavily on the subtleties of sound.

HEARING WITH THE BRAIN

Our ears are simply a conduit for sounds, and they don't do any processing in and of themselves. The sound waves affect the organs in the ear and mechanically transmit those waves to the brain. This is where noise filtering and all other sound processing occurs. So, while you may have physical limitations to your hearing that are governed by your actual ear organs, you can work to sensitize your brain and its interpretation of these sounds. This training can improve how sounds are filtered and distinguished. Here are a few simple exercises you can do to improve your awareness of sounds.

HEARING EXERCISES

1. Opposite Environment – If you generally live in a noisy environment, make sure to allow

yourself periods of silence. Consider getting a pair of noise cancelling headphones or just some ear plugs to enjoy listening to absolutely nothing for a little while. On the other hand, if you live in a generally quiet environment, spice it up by putting on some loud music for a little while.
2. Counting Sounds – Try to count the number of different sounds around you, for example, your refrigerator, a clock, birds chirping, or neighbors talking. Can you hear yourself breathe or hear the wind outside?
3. Noise filtering – Start a conversation with someone in a regular speaking tone. Have someone else add in a distracting noise like relatively loud music and continue carrying on the conversation at the same level. After a while, have them add another distracting background noise and continue carrying on the same conversation.
4. Source Locating – Have a partner move around the room and make a short, distinct noise of some sort. As soon as you hear the noise, point to where you hear it coming from. Have your partner let you know if you got it right, and if not, how close you came. Also, try approximating how far away they are. This may

require some distracting noise when they are moving around the room in order to disguise their footsteps.
5. Copying – Listen to talk radio, a news broadcast, or a podcast, nothing in particular just anything that interests you. Listen intently for a moment and then begin to repeat everything that is said, word for word. Keep up with the speaker, but vary the amount of time you leave between their words and your words. This is a great exercise for the brain as well as the ears.

HEARING MEDITATION

Meditation has been used for thousands of years to increase awareness and can be used prior to echolocation practice to help open the mind and become more sensitive to the intricacies of your soundscape, or the sounds around you. The goal is simply to listen intently to everything around you and process it all at one time. In essence, hear all the sounds around you as if they were all one sound. Essentially, they are.

The vibrations that have come from each object, event, or person culminate in your eardrum as one finite amount of fluctuating air pressure that is then registered by your brain. Your brain will work hard to process this one sound and break it up accordingly, based on where it knows the sounds are coming from. The brain will separate the clock from the birds, from the wind, from people talking, from your own breath, etc. Let's give the brain a break for a moment and just experience the raw input of sound pressure coming into the ears.

First, sit in a comfortable place in a position that suits you – sitting, kneeling, lying down etc. Before trying anything, just take 10 deep, relaxed breaths and let your heart rate slow down as you relax and find comfort in your seat. Then, start listening for all the sounds you can hear. It's okay to focus on the sounds one at a time to start. In fact, you should focus on the loudest sound you can hear, and then find the second loudest. Count as many sounds as you can in the order that you notice them. Once you have found the next slightly quieter sound, listen to it for 20 - 30 seconds and then scan for something even quieter or more distant. This exercise will sensitize your ears and help you increase your awareness of your environment.

After finding as many sounds as possible, try listening to them all at once. Try to stop thinking, "that's the clock" or "there goes another car." Just be mindful and allow them all to congeal as one sound wave and listen to that sound wave. Once you have come to allow all of the sounds to come together, it should seem more like a song than each of these things individually. This song is a representation of the power of the current moment. By listening to this song, you will start to realize the power in every moment throughout your day. Each moment is powerful in its own way, and it is up to you to realize that and make the absolute best of it. Don't spend more than 5 - 10 minutes doing this, because it is easy to lose focus unless you are accustomed to longer meditation.

BEGINNER'S GUIDE TO ECHOLOCATION

In addition to helping improve and sensitize your ears, hearing meditation can also be very rewarding as it can give you a sense of relaxation, focus, and confidence. Being mindful of yourself and your surroundings can eliminate attachment to physical things and emotions that may be connected with people and things around you. Release all hatred, resentment, frustration, longing, pain, and suffering and consider the beauty of the present moment and the *song* that describes it.

SENSITIZING YOUR HEARING USING MUSIC

If you listen to a lot of music, this is a good way to begin sensitizing; however, start listening more intently. Try to pick out every different instrument in a particular song. Begin noticing subtleties such as:

1. Which speaker is each instrument coming from? Or, is it coming from both? This is called *panning*, and often times songs will pan one guitar further to the left speaker and another guitar further to the right. This is done to give the effect that the guitars are in two different places on a stage. Once you've started to pick up on this effect, you should be able to point directly to where each instrument appears to be coming from, which should be somewhere in between the two speakers depending on how much it is panned one way or the other.

2. Determine how *far away* each instrument (including the singer) appears. This is basically accomplished by the recording company by adding more or less echo or reverberation time to the signal. If a longer reverb is added to an instrument, it will give it the effect of being in a large room and possibly far away. If a short

reverb is added, it will give the effect of having very nearby walls and will be closer and more intimate. Generally, vocal tracks have more delay added so that the singer seems closer and more pronounced to the listener.

This is a very simple and very enjoyable method of sensitizing your ears to subtleties. Now you can mellow out after a long day and listen to your favorite tunes knowing that you are becoming a better, more rounded person at the same time.

THE SENSATION OF ECHOLOCATION

Echolocation is a phenomenon that is perceived in different ways by different people. In this book, it is described somewhat analytically. However, it is often better to sensitize to the overall phenomenon as a unique mode of perception in and of itself.

Some people refer to it as a pressure felt on their face. This is referred to as *facial vision* or *facial pressure* and is used, sometimes subconsciously, by many people who have been blind for a long time. Facial pressure is not a different phenomenon than echolocation; it is simply an interpretation of this mode of perception. All people experience the world differently and will describe their experiences in the way that best suits them. Technically, all sounds incur pressure on the face; sound is a wave of pressure that moves through the air and any sound coming toward you is striking your face as well as your ears. Despite the fact that your face doesn't actually detect this pressure, this might be one way to think about it in order to start perceiving objects around you. Many people who have been blind for a long time and have no idea what echolocation is, have some sense of where walls are and they have a sensation if they are about to hit something. That is the sensation of echolocation and that is (eventually) what we will attempt to harness and understand in this book. Other people have been known to characterize the effect of echolocation as air currents around objects, intuition, or simply a presence.

These are all fine characterizations, and you will undoubtedly come up with your own method of describing the sensation of echolocation. In fact, it is recommended that you do so. No two people learn exactly the same way, and everyone is encouraged to learn in their own unique way. If you find a way to describe the sensation in your own terms, it will give you a more intimate level of understanding. And, understanding how your mind works and allowing it to work in this unique way will give you a personalized understanding of this very subtle effect that we're calling echolocation.

EXPERIENCE ECHOLOCATION WHILE RIDING IN A CAR

While riding in the car, leave the passenger's side window open and close all the other windows. This is a good way of directing your attention in one discrete direction. Keep things fairly quiet inside the car. Turn off the radio and cease conversation to make it easier to hear the sounds coming in through the window.

As you pass by objects on the side of the road, it's apparent that they are detectable via sound. Obviously, other passing cars and pedestrians make sounds of their own, but listen for telephone poles, parked cars, or trees that emit no sound of their own. They will sound more like a "whoosh" of wind as you pass by. The sound that these objects seem to emit is actually the sound of your own car reflecting off them and coming back into your window. This works well, because a car engine emits quite a bit of sound that is quite constant and covers a fairly broad spectrum of audio (high tones, mid tones, and low tones). The engine noise is loud from the outside of the car, and is quiet on the inside. The outside car engine noise is apparent when it is reflected into the window.

BEGINNER'S GUIDE TO ECHOLOCATION

This is a very simple way of experiencing echolocation that anyone can do. Certainly this affect is amplified and exaggerated due to the circumstances (loud engine noise and large, fast moving target objects), and standard echolocation will not sound like this, but this method is a good thing to try if you are skeptical about the reality of echolocation. Sound does in fact reflect off silent objects, and that sound is unquestionably detectable.

Try listening more intently to these sounds and determine what kind of object you are passing based on the sound it makes. You'll notice that you can determine a lot about an object by the way it sounds – the size, shape, distance, and even material.

The following are a few descriptions of standard objects you might pass in a car and start to make observations about.

THE SOUND OF A TELEPHONE POLE

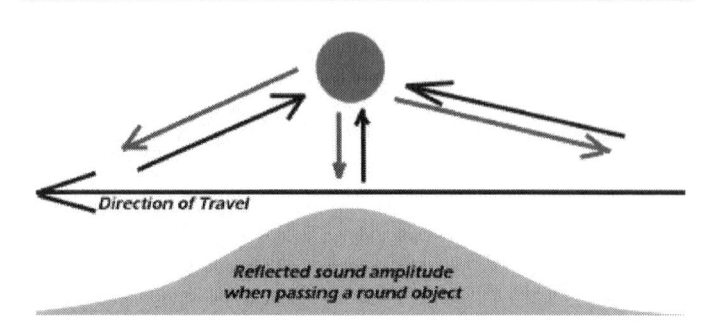

Direction of Travel

Reflected sound amplitude when passing a round object

When sound reaches a round object, it reflects and scatters based on the angle of the surface it hits. Since a telephone pole is round, there is always one part of the surface that is perpendicular to you. As you pass by a pole in a car, the sound reflection pattern can be described as a *swell*. As you approach the pole, you can hear reflections gradually fade in and peak as you pass it, and then fade away evenly. This would be the same for any round object that you are passing along the direction of its curvature. Additionally, sound disperses over distance so the object will be louder the closer you are to it.

THE SOUND OF A MAILBOX

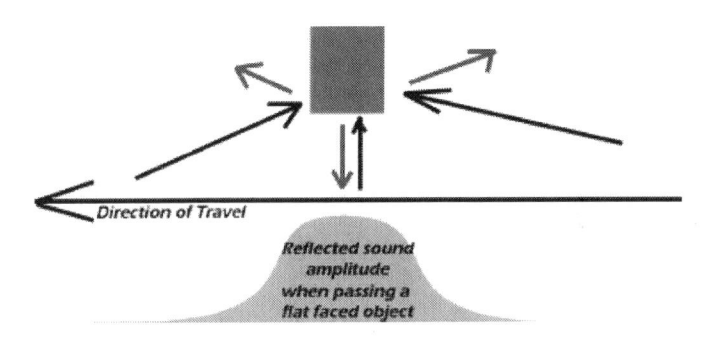

Reflected sound amplitude when passing a flat faced object

The response curve of a mailbox is different from a telephone pole due to its shape. Since they have a flat face, generally parallel with the street, the response curve is more of a square wave. In other words, the reflection of the sound is very apparent when you are directly alongside the flat face, and then drops off quickly once you pass. They have a much briefer presence. As you pass this object, you will get a short steady burst of sound reflected into your window, and then it will quickly disappear. Upon approaching the object, the sound is reflected in other directions, as there are no perpendicular surfaces to direct it back in your direction.

Another interesting observation about metal mailboxes is that the reflected tone is higher than that of a telephone pole or a tree. The higher frequency sound waves are reflected easily by the hard metal surface of the mailbox, whereas the wooden surface of telephone poles and trees absorb some of the higher frequencies.

THE SOUND OF PARKED CARS

Moving cars are easy; they emit their own sound! But, parked cars are unique in that you can recognize the metallic material they are made of because of the higher frequencies they reflect. When frequencies start getting absorbed, usually the higher ones are the first to go since lower frequencies, by nature, travel greater distances. Try to notice the different sounds that cars of different sizes make. Large trucks sound different from small cars. By noticing exaggerated differences, you will eventually be able to identify smaller and smaller differences.

THE SOUND OF FENCING

Flat fencing is generally distinct, switching *on* quickly when you approach and *off* quickly when it ends, and generally remains very constant when you are passing it. Wooden fencing doesn't generally reflect the higher tones while metal fencing will. A picket fence should also be very apparent due to the fluttering response it delivers.

ECHOLOCATION AWARENESS EXERCISE

Another simple exercise to easily experience the effect of echolocation is simply walking from the inside of your house to the outside of your house. While inside and while the environment is fairly quiet, listen to the sounds around you as there is almost always some sort of ambient noise present. Take a few steps through your front door and notice how the sounds change, not just the actual source of the sound (undoubtedly, you will be hearing different sounds like cars and birds as opposed to the refrigerator and a clock) but the qualities of the sound, such as the loudness, pitch, direction, echo, etc.

Generally, when you are inside any building all of the sounds you hear tend to come from several directions. It will be loudest in the actual direction of the object making the sound, but it will also echo off all the walls and objects inside the room. Musicians go to great lengths to eliminate, or at least minimize, sound reflections when recording. It's called *reverb* and it can make things sound completely different.

Each room of a given size and shape has its own unique acoustic signature. The size of a room will dictate which frequencies are most prominent as the distance between two parallel walls creates something called a *standing wave,* which is a sound wave with a wavelength that evenly fits within that dimension. These standing waves will actually appear to be amplified. Additionally, each room will have its own unique reverb based on the distance and angle of all of the walls and items in the room.

Reverb is an effect that we have all experienced, but realizing that this simple effect is actually the sense of echolocation that can be trained and improved to see things in greater and greater detail can be profound.

ECHOLOCATION IN TERMS OF *REVERB*

Let's look for a second at echolocation as it would be viewed by a musician. Every room and every environment, whether it's indoors or outdoors, has its own acoustic signature. These would be known to musicians as that room's reverberant properties, or its *reverb*. Certain rooms are said to have a certain type of reverb. Rooms with hard, flat parallel walls generally are considered to be *live*, whereas rooms with softer (more absorbent) walls that are oddly misshapen have less reverb, and are considered *dead*, meaning that the sound is not as likely to bounce around as much. A *highly reverberant room* is labeled such because the sound waves are likely to bounce off of the walls, sometimes several times before making their way to the listener. This gives the effect that one short tone is stretched out over a longer period of time. Essentially, the reverb is made up of many very quick echoes from nearby objects.

You have undoubtedly experienced and are familiar with certain reverb characteristics. For example, if you are in a quiet environment and you close your eyes and snap your fingers, you will immediately be able to tell if you are in a bathroom, car, or auditorium. A seasoned recording musician could probably guess if the floor was carpeted and what the walls were made of. They don't refer to this as echolocation, but they do have the necessary sensitivity to detect these subtleties.

Audio Technicians work hard to make recording artists sound certain ways based on how they want to be heard. An acoustic folk singer, for instance, has a sound that is very *close* – the studio makes it sound like they are playing in a small room, like a coffee shop, or your own living room. Whereas, the rock band Kiss is made to sound very large and far away as if you were hearing them in a stadium or a large rock concert arena. This is intentional and done primarily with reverb and other effects that are mostly based on echo and sound delay. Reverb is further and more accurately described by the concept of *reverberation time*.

REVERBERATION TIME

The actual difference between a *close* sound and a *far* sound, or a *dead* room and a *live* room, is that of reverberation time. This is the time it takes for the sound from one event (like a clap) to cease after the initial sound has stopped. Between the time that the clap stops and the time that the residual sound in a room stops is the reverberation time. This can vary between 0.3 seconds in a small, carpeted household room, and up to 8 seconds in a cathedral like Notre Dame where sounds become *muddy* when speaking but are designed to be very dramatic sounding for things like pipe organs. A general-purpose auditorium has a reverberation time of about 1.5 - 2.5 seconds.

During this time, what is happening is that the initial sound is travelling outward in all directions from its source, in this case, the hands clapping. The shortest distance between two points is of course, a straight line; therefore, the first sound you hear comes directly from the hands. Sometime after that sound reaches you, the sound travels to the nearest wall, is reflected off it, and then it too comes to meet your ears. Additionally, it travels to the furthest wall in the room, reflects off that and it also makes its way to your ears. Not only that, in many cases, the sound will reflect off of three, four, five, or more walls or objects and still make it to your ears with enough volume to be audible.

Travelling outward in three-dimensional space, the sound is striking, reflecting, and continuing on to your ears in an infinite number of directions. Despite the fact that you may not be a professional recording musician, simply knowing that this effect takes place is a concept

BEGINNER'S GUIDE TO ECHOLOCATION

you should be familiar with when starting to train in echolocation.

BEGINNER'S GUIDE TO ECHOLOCATION

PART 4

SIGNALS FOR ECHOLOCATING

CLICKS, CLAPS, AMBIENTS,

AND OTHER SIGNALS

PASSIVE VERSUS ACTIVE ECHOLOCATION

If you have been blind most of your life and are familiar with some of the basic sensations of echolocation, for instance, you can tell what size room you are in, or you get a strange sensation right before you crash into a wall, you are using what is known as *passive echolocation*.

Passive echolocation is the sensitization to commonly occurring sound events such as your footsteps, cane tip, the swishing of your clothes, the sound of your voice, or even your own breath. You are sensing changes in how these sounds reflect off objects, and that is what gives you that sensation or intuition. It's good to use passive echolocation as this will harbor a high level of sensitivity for your ears. However, in order to start using echolocation with another level of clarity, one should implement *active echolocation*.

Active echolocation is the use of a specific signal sound that is designed and optimized for reflecting off objects. It is a sound that you know and are familiar with and will be able to distinguish the subtleties of how it changes after it interacts with obstacles. Generally, this signal sound is a very short, high-pitched, penetrating sound. For most proficient echolocators, this sound is made by creating a clicking sound with the mouth. The reason the mouth is used is because it is with you wherever you go. The mouth, being part of the head, is also quite close to the ears, which means that sound travelling outward from it, and thus being reflected off of obstacles, will be travelling directly *from* and directly *to* the ears.

This will be critical in accurately determining the location of the obstacle. If the source sound, or signal, were to be offset from the ears by a greater distance, it would be much harder to judge the accurate direction from which an echo returns. Another reason the mouth is a good tool is that, because of its shape, it actually does not emit sound equally in all directions. The loudest sound waves, or the sound waves with the most pressure and energy, will be emitted directly in front of your face. This is optimal given the shape and placement of your ears with respect to this signal.

PASSIVE ECHOLOCATION SIGNALS

Passive signaling during echolocation involves listening to the ambient noises in the room and interpreting them. It has its pros, such as not being intrusive or noticeable. These sounds can be:

- People talking
- A running fan
- Footsteps
- Cane tapping
- Clothes rubbing against each other
- Hands rubbing together
- Breathing
- Machinery & clocks

One of the downfalls of these sounds is the fact that their source is potentially unfamiliar and therefore any sound that is reflected to the listener contains information that might not be interpreted entirely correctly.

These sounds can, however, be used to make broad observations such as the size of a room or proximity to a flat wall. If you have been blind for some time these may be signals that you use on a regular basis to understand where you are, and what is going on around you. This is a good starting point, and if you do use these methods, you have experienced the tip of the iceberg in the world of echolocation.

Children who are born blind or lose their vision at a very young age have been known to create loud noises like screaming, stomping, yelling, clapping or banging on loud objects. This is a method they are using to learn about their environment. This behavior is often not encouraged because people don't understand what the child is trying to accomplish, but if we were able to recognize these strategies being implemented by children and encourage them to explore them further, they would be ahead of the game in the field of echolocation as they grow older.

PROPERTIES OF A GOOD CLICK SIGNAL

To implement *active echolocation*, it's important to first come up with a good quality signal or click. Each practitioner will have different clicks that are more comfortable to them. Generally, the more familiar you are with a sound the better it will work for you. There are many fundamental qualities of a click signal that make the signal better suited for echolocation.

FREQUENCY

The frequency of a signal governs the resolution, in that a shorter wavelength (higher frequency) will give you more definition as to what it has bounced off. Low frequency waves, since they have a longer wavelength, are not as distinct. It has been suggested that the region of 3kHz is a good frequency for echolocating.

However, a broad distribution of frequencies would also be desirable such that if one discreet frequency does not respond against a certain surface, another slightly different frequency will. If you create a signal that only includes one discreet frequency, it is likely that it will be absorbed by some particular material. Luckily, it is *very* hard to create a signal containing only one frequency, except by laboratory equipment. Even a simple finger snap is made up of a large spectrum of frequencies (see next section).

By creating a signal that includes a distribution of frequencies, or a spectrum of some high tones, some mid tones, and some lower tones, if some frequencies are absorbed by an object, others will be reflected by it and thus will be detected when you hear the echo. This will also help you to determine the construct of objects better as that is generally determined by the tones that naturally resonate off the object.

VOLUME

The sound must be loud enough to stand out over ambient noise. This will obviously depend on the environment you are in, and there are several different signals that can be used in quiet environments and others in loud environments. Alternatively, if you are in an environment that is very loud, but consists mostly of mid-range tones – perhaps a restaurant – there is still a good likelihood that you will be able to successfully distinguish a high-level signal sound through the loud ambient noise.

CLARITY

This is probably one of the most, if not *the* most important property of the signal sound. It is critical that after the sound is made, there are no artifacts of the signal source still emitting sound. In other words, the sound must stop abruptly so that the reverberations can be clearly heard. If the sound were to taper off at all, this small amount of sound would tend to cover up the reverberations, or at least create a confusing blend of signals. Examples of a sound that would taper off and provide an unclear echolocation signal is an "AH" sound or a "CH" sound. Sometimes these simple sounds are made instinctively by blind children when they are realizing the existence of echolocation and trying to gain information about their environment by shouting or stomping their feet.

DIRECTION

If the signal is omni-directional (in other words, if it is the same volume in all directions as emitted from the source), it will be more difficult to determine the direction from which it is being reflected, and thus where the object is that is doing the reflecting. When using a click for echolocation, we get only very brief images of our surroundings that last for the duration of the click plus the reverberation time. When learning echolocation, it is best to focus on one direction at a time instead of the big picture. Creating a directional click signal will help *focus* the sound toward an obstacle and hence the response from the obstacle in order to glean as much information about that particular thing as possible.

ALIGNMENT

This is the concept of having three items: the ears, the signal source, and the target object all in relatively straight alignment. For example, if, in an attempt to echolocate an object directly in front of you, you were to stretch out your arm to the side and use a clicking device or your fingers, the sound coming from your hand (held out at your side) would bounce off the object (in front of you) at a different angle causing the response signal from that object to be abnormal or slanted. If you align your signal (say your snapping fingers) with both your ears and your target object, the sound waves will travel directly from your hand to the object and directly back to your ears. This is the reason it is often encouraged that people use a click or sound made by the mouth for precise echolocation. This provides good control and consistency for the source signal, and therefore will provide consistent responses from obstacles.

BEGINNER'S GUIDE TO ECHOLOCATION

VARIOUS CLICKING TECHNIQUES

Generally, when performing active echolocation, a click sound is made with the mouth as the signal sound or the sound that will be reflected off objects in order to create the ever-important reverb that we have been discussing. Since everyone learns differently and everyone's ears and mouths are constructed slightly differently, I would say there is no particular way to click that works best for everyone. So, try out the different methods and make up your own techniques that work best for you. Here are a few descriptions of clicking noises that you might explore. While you're learning, keep in mind that when clicking it is generally best to allow a few seconds in between clicks in order for the brain to process the information.

THE CLUCK

The *cluck* is made by lightly pressing the tip of the tongue against the roof of the mouth and then breaking the vacuum and smacking your tongue against the floor of your mouth. This is deemed to be a poor signal by World Access for the Blind due to the lack of clarity. It's said that it provides skewed, slanted or out of focus images. Making this sound actually causes several different clicks and sounds spaced very close to one another due to the nature of the way the tongue and mouth interact.

THE GIDDYUP

This one is made by breaking the vacuum and drawing air in between the sides of the tongue and the molars, and is commonly used to communicate with horses to get them to giddyup. By nature, this signal, is produced at the sides of the mouth, and therefore is emitted away from the sides of the head. This is interesting in that we can send the signal to either one side or the other, but it is more difficult to send the signal directly to the front with this method.

HERE KITTY CLICK

This click is made by putting the tip of the tongue on the roof of the mouth or on the back of the front teeth and pulling it away to make the classic "tsk tsk" sound as if to say "here kitty" or "shame on you." This can be a fairly effective click in close, quiet environments, because it is comprised of various frequencies with a good deal of "high-end", and it can be made several times per second. Although it is generally taught to leave a second of two of *breathing room* in between clicks in order for reverberations to subside and for the brain to finish processing. This is, however, a very low-volume click and will not be effective outdoors or in wide-open environments.

BLADE POP

This is commonly used among adept echolocators. It is very crisp, clear, and loud when done properly, but is a bit more difficult to learn. It is made by putting the *meaty*, central part of the tongue or the *blade* up into the roof of the mouth, creating suction and then pulling the tongue back toward the throat to make the click. The tip of the tongue is not involved in this click. The sound from this click comes directly out the front of the mouth and it's easy to get a fairly high tone by widening the mouth. Because of its clarity and volume, this is a very good click for locating objects directly in front of you as well as beside or even behind you. The clarity of this tone is unmatched by the other tones described in this chapter and most echolocation specialists encourage the use of nothing but this particular click.

THE "*SSHH*" SOUND

This is a signal often taught to children and beginners as it is very familiar and easy to make. The frequency response of this signal, as we will see in the next section, is quite flat and provides a broad spectrum of frequencies making it good for reflecting off many different surfaces. Even though this is not recommended for active echolocation practice, it can be helpful when learning the basic concepts.

OTHER SIGNALS

Other things that people use are a basic finger snap, handclap, or clicking device such as a pet trainer or bottle cap. It should be mentioned that these loud clicking devices and methods are not recommended for indoor use or effective for close obstacles. Generally, a clicking device or handclap is better suited for identifying objects greater than 3 yards or 9 feet away. Often times if an adept echolocator is outside and becomes disoriented they may utilize a hand clap to identify large distant objects such as buildings, bridges, groves of trees etc. Of course, creating loud sounds close to your ears is not recommended for the safety of your ears. Another thing to mention for use in very quiet environments is rubbing the tips of the fingers together to achieve a very high-pitched sound that is close to white noise. It is helpful to have dry skin on the fingers for this. As discussed in the previous section, any signal made with the hands should be aligned between the target object and the ears.

THE SCIENCE OF A SIGNAL

To better understand the spectrum of sounds provided by different echolocation signals, I've provided some spectrum analyses of them for a closer look. To understand something as simple as a finger snap to this level of detail will also help with sensitization and will give you an appreciation for everything that is going on during these simple sound events.

What is spectrum analysis? By taking a sample of a certain sound over time, we can computationally analyze how these sounds are constructed and which frequencies are present. A spectrum analysis will give us a plot of the sound pressure level along the entire spectrum of sound, from 20Hz to 20,000Hz. It makes it easy to tell how much *high end* or *low end* a certain sound has. By doing this, the subtle differences between two different signal sounds becomes increasingly apparent.

Even if this doesn't make complete sense and you don't fully appreciate the scientific aspect of a signal, that's okay. It's at least good to know that a signal is made up of many constituents. Somewhere in the back of your mind, you will have this information and maybe you will

BEGINNER'S GUIDE TO ECHOLOCATION

find an application for it during your journey of becoming proficient in echolocation.

The signals described and shown below have been recorded in high fidelity in a completely *dead* environment, without any reverb present. However, based on your own biometrics (the shape of your mouth, fingers, etc.) these responses will be slightly different for everyone.

SPECTRUM ANALYSIS OF A *FINGER SNAP*

Providing a broad spectrum of frequencies throughout the audible range from 20 to 20,000 Hz, this signal has a good amount of response in the low end from 20 to 2000 Hz. However, there are 8-9 peaks present from 3000 to 9000 Hz which provide the majority of the response.

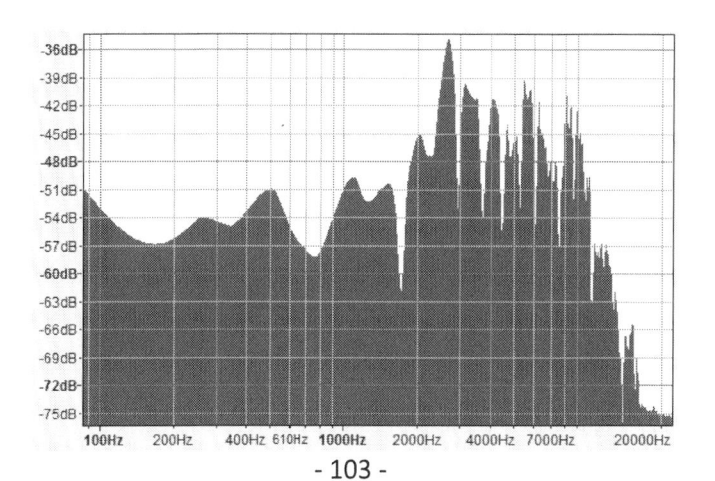

SPECTRUM ANALYSIS OF THE *CLUCK*

This signal has a very flat response from 20 to 1000Hz with a peak at 1500Hz. There is a significant dip at 3000Hz, a few more very small peaks between 4000 and 9000Hz, and then it drops off above that.

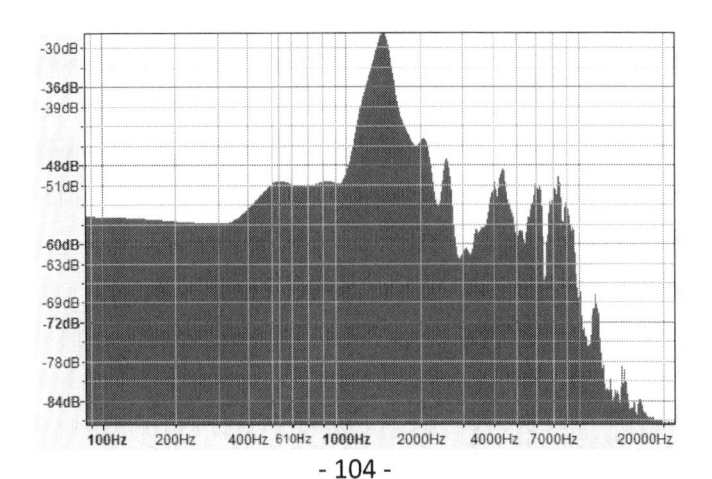

SPECTRUM ANALYSIS OF *HERE KITTY*

With very little response on the low end, this signal starts to gradually ramp up at about 500Hz and peaks around 4500Hz with additional significant peaks at 7000 and 8000Hz. It tapers off quickly after 9000Hz and provides a minimal response above that level.

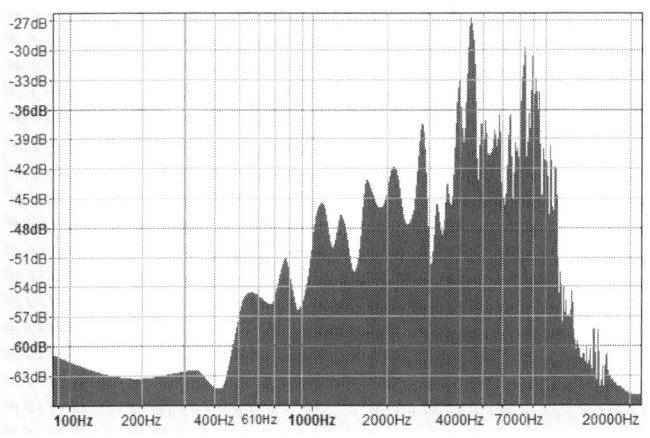

BEGINNER'S GUIDE TO ECHOLOCATION

SPECTRUM ANALYSIS OF THE *GIDDYUP*

This signal has a fairly low response on the low end of the spectrum, with a small peak around 100Hz and another around 1000Hz. There is a quick rise at around 2000Hz and three peaks from 5000 to 7000Hz where the majority of the signal is focused. This signal drops off quickly above 9000Hz.

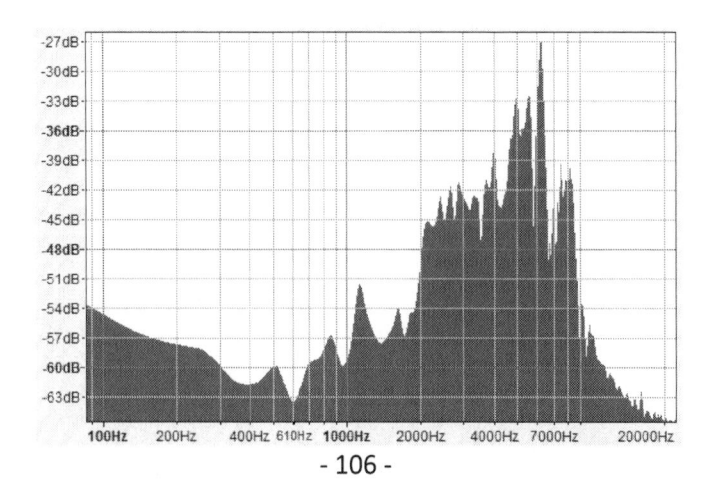

BEGINNER'S GUIDE TO ECHOLOCATION

SPECTRUM ANALYSIS OF THE *BLADE POP*

This signal provides a surprisingly flat frequency response. This means that the strength of the signal is quite evenly distributed throughout a large portion of the spectrum. From 20 to 1500Hz the signal is fairly uniform. A large peak exists from 1500 to 2500Hz and above that additional peaks exist at 5000 and 6000Hz.

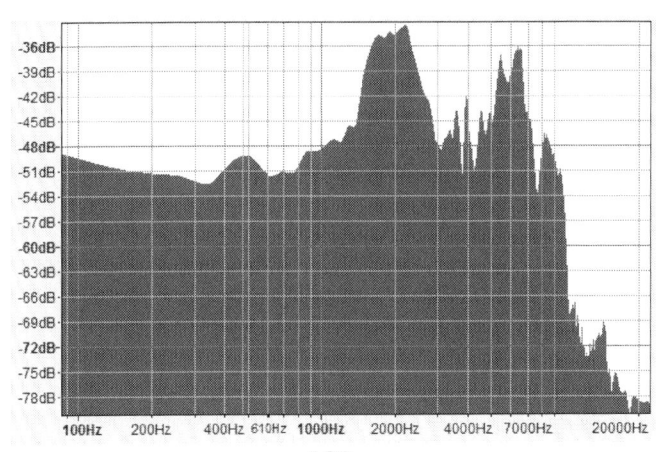

BEGINNER'S GUIDE TO ECHOLOCATION

SPECTRUM ANALYSIS OF "SSHH"

Three prominent peaks exist here at 3000 to 6000 and 7000Hz. A good amount of low-end response is present from 20 to 300Hz, but there is a sizeable dip in response between 400 and 1500Hz.

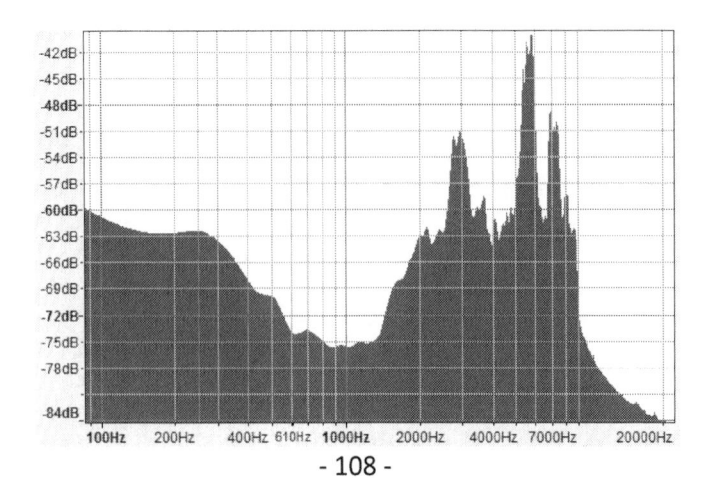

BEGINNER'S GUIDE TO ECHOLOCATION

SPECTRUM ANALYSIS OF RUBBING FINGERS TOGETHER

With a lower amplitude overall, this signal starts with a good response on the low end and tapers off gradually as it approaches 3500 Hz. A large, wide peak is present from 5000 to 10,000Hz.

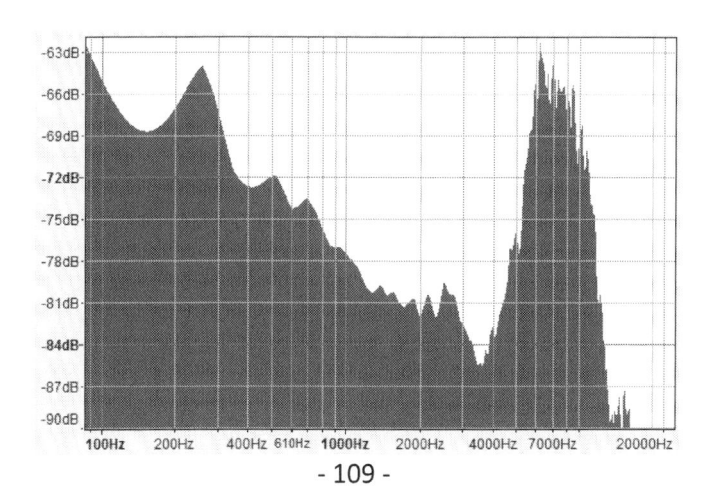

BEGINNER'S GUIDE TO ECHOLOCATION

SPECTRUM ANALYSIS OF *TRUE WHITE NOISE*

White noise is simply a randomly generated wave that includes all audible frequencies. Thus, it makes sense that this signal has a very flat response all the way from 20 to 20,000Hz. White noise is not a natural sound and cannot be made by humans, although the "sshh" sound is similar.

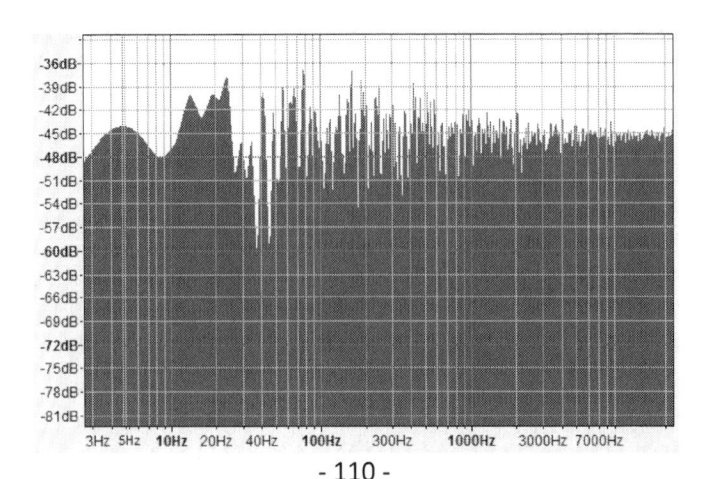

WHY A 3KHZ SIGNAL IS OPTIMAL FOR ECHOLOCATION

Below is a representation of the human hearing threshold which gives us a good idea why the 3 kilohertz (kHz) range is a good signal to use for echolocation.

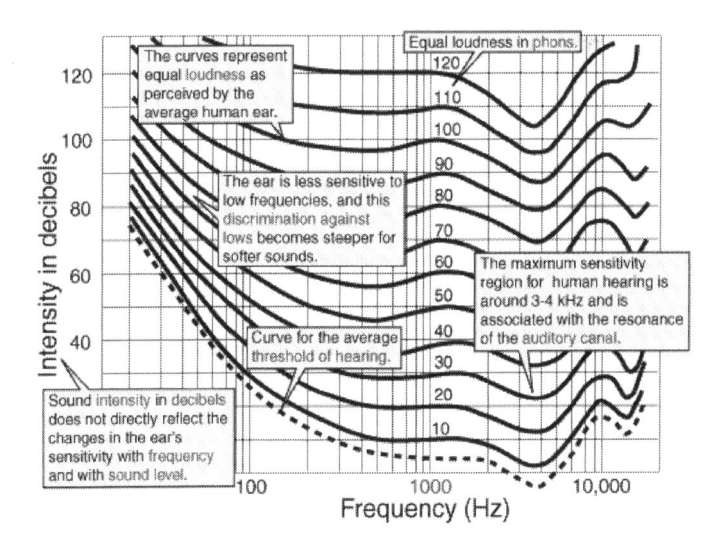

[Figure: Equal loudness curves (in phons) showing intensity in decibels vs frequency (Hz). Annotations: "The curves represent equal loudness as perceived by the average human ear." "The ear is less sensitive to low frequencies, and this discrimination against lows becomes steeper for softer sounds." "Curve for the average threshold of hearing." "Sound intensity in decibels does not directly reflect the changes in the ear's sensitivity with frequency and with sound level." "The maximum sensitivity region for human hearing is around 3-4 kHz and is associated with the resonance of the auditory canal."]

Source: http://hyperphysics.phy-astr.gsu.edu/hbase/sound/eqloud.html

This chart is plotting the intensity in decibels that is audible by the human ear at different frequencies along the audible spectrum of sound. Additionally, the different lines represent different signal loudness levels.

At lower frequencies and lower loudness levels, it becomes increasingly difficult to differentiate between tones. The lower tones, near 20 Hertz are only audible once they reach approximately 75 decibels (dB), which means that a low tone needs to be far more powerful to be perceived.

There is a consistent dip around 3kHz where it is indicated that softer sounds are perceived just as well as other frequency tones of the same loudness. As signals get higher in frequency, it is required again that they be of greater loudness in order to be perceived at the same level.

This has to do with the construction of the human ear canal. A 3kHz frequency resonates nicely in a 2.4cm tube at body temperature, which is the average size of an ear canal.

We have to remember, however, that a single frequency tone is not *entirely* optimal due to other circumstances. For instance, a 3kHz tone may be completely absorbed by an object. Drapery appears to absorb these frequencies very efficiently, as well as upholstered benches according to the absorption coefficient chart in Part 5. These objects may be more easily seen using lower frequencies of which they absorb less. For this reason, it is important to choose a signal that consists of a broad spectrum of frequencies.

CLICKING DEVICES AND ALTERNATIVES

Handheld clickers may be used for echolocation; you can use a Snapple-type cap, or a pet training clicker. First thing's first, you must get used to the sound of the clicker. Play with it as much as you can, every day. Eventually you will be able to recognize it easily and at this point, you will have learned many of the subtleties of the sound.

Don't forget that it's important that your signal be aligned with your target properly in order to avoid confusing responses.

It can be helpful to create a barrier directly between the clicking source and your ear. This could be your other hand (as if saying "Stop"), a notebook, or a small object you're carrying. This will block the original signal and prevent it from going directly to your ear and will make the response signal more prominent. Be careful that your object is not too large as it can block the response signal as well, making the image unclear.

When using a clicker, pause briefly between the press and the release of the button. This will give the reverberations time to subside and will avoid confusion allowing your brain to process all of the reverberations before hearing another click.

FINDING *YOUR* SIGNAL

Whatever you use for a click has to be a sound you're familiar with. You know the sound of your front door and you know the sound of a soda or beer can being cracked open. Sounds like these are powerful because they instinctively trigger thoughts and emotions prior to you actively conceptualizing their source. The sound you use for echolocation should be similar to this so that you are familiar enough with it to recognize the very subtle variations that are necessary for echolocation.

It has to be consistent. Whatever it is, try not to change it too often unless you're experimenting. One sound may return different reverberant characteristics than another in the same environment.

You have to be able to hear it. It doesn't make a lot of sense to make a sound that will be difficult to hear. This implies that the sound wave must have enough energy to return to your ear and still be recognizable. This also has to do with the environment you're in. It's best to find something that is versatile and can be used in many environments. If your signal has very little low-end response and all high-end, it might be difficult to hear in an environment comprised of many high level frequencies as nothing will stand out as unique.

Other things to keep in mind are that higher frequencies have a higher energy than lower frequencies and therefore will return information more effectively. They will also give you better resolution since the wavelength is shorter.

BEGINNER'S GUIDE TO ECHOLOCATION

BEGINNER'S GUIDE TO ECHOLOCATION

PART 5

ECHOLOCATION LESSONS

BEGINNER'S GUIDE TO ECHOLOCATION

"SHARPEN YOUR BLADE. FROM THE TIME YOU WAKE UP UNTIL THE TIME YOU GO TO BED."

SIFU SHI YAN MING
ABBOTT OF THE USA
SHAOLIN TEMPLE

SEEING SOMETHING VERSUS NOTHING

Many of the awareness exercises and methods of experiencing echolocation previously discussed will already put you on the path of seeing something via echolocation. The next step is to identify the sound you hear with a particular object. It's best to start with a hard flat object such as a book or a piece of cardboard or wood. This lesson will be done in close proximity, so you shouldn't need anything larger than 10" x 10" to start with. A standard size textbook would work well.

1. It's best to locate yourself outside, away from large objects. If that is not possible, locate yourself in a carpeted room with lots of soft furniture and window treatments. This will provide a very *dead* room in terms of reverb and will make it easier to distinguish small subtleties.
2. First, simply make your signal noise. Listen and get accustomed to it in your environment. This is like a calibration.
3. Next, move the object in front of your face and continue to make your signal.
4. If you are having trouble hearing the difference, try the "sshh" signal as that is often used by

children and provides a good response for beginners.
5. If you are still having trouble, make sure the object is very close to your face when it is there and completely away when it is gone. Moving it only a little bit will be less obvious than completely removing it from view.
6. If you cannot detect a presence, try moving it to and from your view very quickly while using the "sshh" sound. Simply slide the object in front of your face and then slide it away to the side. Doing this quickly will create a quick change in the sound which will be more easily detected.
7. What you experience – *whatever* you experience – is echolocation. It cannot be explained in a book, and as previously discussed, it will be described differently by everyone who experiences it. Scientifically speaking, the frequency, spectral pattern, and reverberations have been altered by the presence of this object. Become familiar with this phenomenon and give it your own unique definition and description.

The next step to this exercise will be having a partner hold the object in front of you and for you to tell them when it is there, and when they have removed it.

RIGHT VERSUS LEFT

To begin determining direction, you will need to be able to differentiate between objects to your right and objects to your left.

1. Using a partner, start by performing the above exercise something versus nothing toward one side of your head. Perhaps not directly on the side, but out in front of you to the right or left at about a 45-degree angle.
2. For this exercise, the flat surface of the object should always be facing directly toward you. This will ensure that the strongest, clearest response is reflected back toward you.
3. It is important that the object you are using does not make any noise of its own, such as the pages of a magazine. It's also important that the person holding the object does not scratch or manipulate it in such a way that makes any sound. This will defeat the purpose of the exercise.
4. Once you can clearly tell when the object is present and when it's not, try it on the other side.
5. Get used to both sides and then have your partner surprise you. After a short period of

BEGINNER'S GUIDE TO ECHOLOCATION

training, you should be able to easily determine where the object is.

ABOVE VERSUS BELOW

This is slightly more difficult. The ears are positioned on the side of the head, so right to left differentiation is easier than up and down. Right to left relies on the difference in amplitude or volume between the signals coming in each ear. The ability to differentiate between sounds from above and sounds from below relies primarily on the shape of the ear and the ear canal making it a bit more ambiguous. However, your brain already knows how to do this, so trust it.

1. Have your partner make a sound in front of your face, but slightly above it at about a 45-degree angle upward. Tell them to rub their fingers together gently to create a quiet sound.
2. Have them move their hand below your face, to about a 45-degree angle and make the same subtle sound. This will give you a frame of reference for echolocating to these two positions.
3. Now have them hold up your hard flat object in these two locations. Use your signal and learn to sense its direction the same way you sensed the direction of the sound they made with their hand. At this point, have them tell you which position it's in.

4. The next obvious step is for them to randomly change the location of the object and have you distinguish the location by pointing up or down. It's important that they confirm your answer so that you can learn when you make a mistake.
5. If this exercise proves to be difficult, simply move the object closer to your face until it becomes apparent. From there you can gradually have your partner move it away as you become more comfortable.

LEARNING TO GAUGE DISTANCE

When learning to gauge distance, we're using neither the difference in volume between the two ears nor the shape of the ear canals to determine the location of the sound. Now, we will be utilizing the changes in echo length or the reverb characteristics of the object.

1. When beginning this exercise, start very close to your face. Move the object away slowly to a known distance – about an arm's length.
2. Get used to the variations in sound due to the change in distance on your own.
3. Next, you guessed it, grab your partner and have them do the same thing for you.
4. Get comfortable with a known distance (from very close to 3 feet away).
5. Next, ask your partner to pick two new distances (3 feet away to about 10 feet away). Make sure your object is large enough to be distinguished from this distance. It might be best to start with something rather large like a 4' x 4' piece of cardboard.

CALIBRATING TO ANGLED SURFACES

Now that you have become familiar with hard flat objects, it's time to learn what angled or slanted surfaces look like.

1. Returning to the Right Versus Left lesson concept, use your flat panel or object and move it side to side in front of you while clicking.
2. This time, be sure to keep the object facing the same direction. Do not reorient it so that the flat surface is always facing you, simply move it side to side, as if it was up against a wall.
3. Notice how the response of your signal changes as the object moves back and forth. Since the flat surface is no longer perpendicular to the direction of the sound, it reflects it back to you differently. In fact, you will notice that the sound it reflects back to you (or the response) is much softer when it is off to one side.
4. Picture shooting a squirt gun or a hose at the flat panel when it is directly in front of you. You will probably get wet since the water will bounce off the flat object and splash back onto you.

5. Now picture shooting a squirt gun at the object when it is off to your side. The water will still hit and bounce off the object, but it is not likely to be directed back at you. The same is the case for sound. The response is much lower because the majority of the sound from your signal is reflected off in a different direction.
6. Minute textures in the material of the object do in fact allow some of the sound to be reflected back toward you. So, even though the object is more difficult to hear at this angle, it is still possible and only takes more sensitization to make it achievable.
7. Play with the angle of the object when it is off to your side. Try turning it to face you, and then turn it away so that the sound bounces off it. Try varying the amount of angle until you can no longer see the object. For a very thin object, like a piece of cardboard, it may disappear completely; however, you may still be able to distinguish the edge of a textbook, for instance.
8. Keep getting more accustomed to sensing the angle of the surface. When you're ready, have your partner hold the object somewhere in front of you, either straight in front, or to one side or the other, and at any angle.

BEGINNER'S GUIDE TO ECHOLOCATION

Now slowly and carefully determine the location and the angle of the object and move so that you are directly facing it. Remember, no cheating by using your hands or other clues! Have your partner verify your success.

CALIBRATING TO ROUND OBJECTS

Where sound reflects off a flat surface differently depending on the angle you approach it, round objects, like telephone poles and trees reflect sound exactly the same – in other words they *look* exactly the same – no matter which angle you approach them from.

This lesson will exploit the concept of changing your angle to your target to identify its shape.

1. If you have a large coffee can, that can work well as a target. Otherwise, choose something else that is at least 12 inches long with a diameter of at least 10 inches. This will be a very easy object to see. If you have nothing that you can hold that is this shape, use a tree or telephone poll for training.
2. Start with the previous lessons to calibrate to a flat and angled surface, and as in those lessons now move the rounded target side to side along that same path.
3. Notice how the response from the round object is quite different from the flat surface. Since the object is round and the edges have very steep angles, the sound on those edges will be primarily reflected in other directions. This

curvature can make the rounded object *seem* a bit smaller than it actually is. The strongest signal will come from the centerline of the object, but sound reflecting off the sloped edges may seem to fade out.
4. Notice that moving the object side to side does not change the amount of sound reflected; only the position, since the angles of reflection will remain unchanged between you and the object.

LEARNING TO DISTINGUISH MATERIALS

One of the modes of perception that is completely unique to echolocation is that of being able to distinguish the difference between hard and soft objects, between smooth and textured objects, and even metal and wood objects.

The importance of having a signal with a broad spectrum of frequencies now becomes crucial. Different frequencies respond differently against different surfaces and materials. Sound can be reflected, absorbed, or diffused.

Hard surfaces like the ones we've been using in previous lessons will reflect sound quite well.

Softer materials like carpet, pillows, upholstered furniture, and other people will absorb sound to varying degrees. When sound is absorbed, it simply means that the echo will be quieter when it returns to your ears. It will sound like the same distance, but since these objects absorb more of the sound, and hence reflect less of the sound, they will be more ambiguous to detect.

BEGINNER'S GUIDE TO ECHOLOCATION

Textured materials will also act to diffuse or scatter the sound. This means that the sound will not necessarily bounce directly off the surface in the direction you might expect it to, but it will bounce in other seemingly random directions changing the response signal slightly.

In order to realize these subtleties, try the following:

1. Find suitable target objects of different materials, such as:
2. Hard, flat objects such as those used in previous lessons.
3. Soft, flat objects such as a flat throw pillow, sheet of foam, or other cushion.
4. Hard, textured objects such as tree bark or a computer keyboard.
5. First, calibrate to your hard flat object at a very close proximity. Move it toward and away from your face between 3 and 12 inches while echolocating.
6. Now swap for the softer object. Within the same range just notice the differences between the hard and the soft object. Keep swapping back and forth and getting more familiar with not necessarily each object on its own, but the difference between the two. If it is difficult to notice a difference, try leaving the flat object in

place and moving the soft object in front of it. There should be a noticeable difference as the hard object becomes muffled.
7. Continue this for the textured material. The close proximity of this lesson will help to exaggerate the subtle differences between these materials, and you can at least get a fundamental understanding of what to listen for. As you improve your skill, you will be able to refer back to these sensations when sighting objects at a greater distance.

FREQUENCY ABSORPTION CHARACTERISTICS OF A VARIETY OF MATERIALS

In order to understand a topic fully, it's important to deviate sometimes and uncover bits of data that are not necessarily contributing toward our physical training or implementation, but instead, add to our overall understanding of a subject. Whether or not you actively utilize this information during your echolocation practice is not important; however, it is important to understand and acknowledge it.

In this case, I would like to take a look at how different materials absorb different frequencies. This will help you to understand how softer items, like upholstered furniture, might differ from doors and how doors differ from concrete. The numbers listed in this chart are the absorption coefficients of these materials.

To give you an idea of how it works, carpet, the first item on the list, has an absorption coefficient of 0.01 for 125Hz frequencies. That means that it will only absorb 1% of a tone at a frequency of 125Hz. It will absorb 2% of a 250Hz tone, 6% of a 500Hz tone, 15% of a 1kHz tone, 25% of a 2kHz tone, and 45% of a 4kHz tone. Of course, if 45% of a tone is absorbed by the material, the remaining 55% of the tone will be reflected. Essentially, the lower the absorption coefficient, the more reflected sound it will yield. Something with a large absorption coefficient, like pleated drapes or occupied seats will be more difficult to see.

The reason we begin learning echolocation using hard flat objects is because things like glass only absorb 2 - 3% of most frequencies and are therefore very reflective, or responsive, while things like upholstery and people absorb at least 25% of most frequencies and up to half of some of the higher frequencies.

The information in the following chart is from the SAE Institute for Audio Engineering.

BEGINNER'S GUIDE TO ECHOLOCATION

Material	125 Hz	250 Hz	500 Hz	1 kHz	2 kHz	4 kHz
Carpet	0.01	0.02	0.06	0.15	0.25	0.45
Concrete	0.01	0.02	0.04	0.06	0.08	0.1
Marble	0.01	0.01	0.01	0.01	0.02	0.02
Benches (wooden, empty)	0.1	0.09	0.08	0.08	0.08	0.08
Benches (wooden, occupied)	0.5	0.56	0.66	0.76	0.8	0.76
Seats (upholstered)	0.49	0.66	0.8	0.88	0.82	0.7
Seats (occupied)	0.6	0.74	0.88	0.96	0.93	0.85
Brick	0.03	0.03	0.03	0.04	0.05	0.07
Concrete (coarse)	0.36	0.44	0.31	0.29	0.39	0.25

BEGINNER'S GUIDE TO ECHOLOCATION

Material	125 Hz	250 Hz	500 Hz	1 kHz	2 kHz	4 kHz
Concrete (painted)	0.1	0.05	0.06	0.07	0.09	0.08
Doors	0.1	0.07	0.05	0.04	0.04	0.04
Glass	0.18	0.06	0.04	0.03	0.02	0.02
Drapery (flat)	0.04	0.05	0.11	0.18	0.3	0.35
Drapery (pleated)	0.14	0.35	0.53	0.75	0.7	0.6
People	0.22	0.3	0.38	0.42	0.45	0.45
Water or ice	0.008	0.008	0.013	0.015	0.02	0.025

MAKE THE SENSATION YOUR OWN

As always, you're encouraged to make your own observations about the subtle differences between the responses during echolocation. If you get a certain feeling or sense that allows you to draw parallels between the sound and the hardness of the object, notice that sensation and try to use it to improve your skill. Maybe the response from softer objects just sounds softer; maybe it seems like it goes deeper into the soft object; maybe you can correlate your perception of this object with a word like squishy or thick. Maybe the hard object seems more bouncy or alive. It's important to utilize these unique and creative words to make this experience very personal, as no two people will ever learn this skill the same way.

If these words don't come to mind automatically, don't force them. Maybe a certain texture comes to mind, a smell, or even a color. It's best to keep an open mind to all possibilities and to treat each new sensation as if it is brand new. This is similar to a child's mind when learning to walk. Children are naturally very good learners because they are open to all methods of learning. As we grow older, having spent years and years building paradigms about the best way to learn, or the right way to learn, we sometimes lose touch with the creative learning process and therefore eliminate much of our own potential. In order to practice this creative learning process, sometimes it requires us to forget everything we know and to think like a young child.

In the mind of the expert there are many possibilities; in the mind of the beginner they are infinite.

LOCATING A DOORWAY

Let's start putting some other basic echolocation skills into practice. The following exercises should be done without any assistance. If you generally use a cane, bring it close to your body and hold it vertically; use it only as a precaution. If you are partially sighted, find a good blindfold that does not allow any light through and does not cover your ears.

1. Stand 3 - 4 feet in front of an open doorway. If possible, the door should be part of a flat wall and it should be fairly clear of obstructions on either side. Make sure there are not too many distracting noises surrounding you; it's certainly easier if it's a very quiet environment. It's also important that the doorway does not have a threshold; this will be a dead giveaway later on.
2. Listen. Take notice of any ambient noise around you. Notice how these ambient noises change as you turn your head. Address the doorway and make the signal noise of your choosing. Turn your head back and forth to click in the direction of both sides of the doorway. Step forward toward the doorway and observe the changes.

BEGINNER'S GUIDE TO ECHOLOCATION

3. Finding the door. Step all the way through the door and notice the changes in sounds from one room to the next. Try to determine when you are exactly inside the doorjamb by listening. Try to hear if you are closer to one side than the other side. Remember to keep turning your head. Focus on one ear at a time. What are the differences? If you think you've made it, grab onto the doorjamb to see how you've done.

NAVIGATING A FAMILIAR ENVIRONMENT

Now that you've got a basic understanding of the concepts and sensations of echolocation, it's time to put it to use in a practical application setting.

1. Use an environment you are completely comfortable with such as your own home.
2. Pick a quiet time of day and dedicate some time to practice.
3. It's important when you've dedicated time to practicing echolocating that you eliminate dependencies on other things like your eyes, your cane, and even your hands. If you want to protect yourself, keep your hands up but keep them very close to you and do not reach out for things.
4. Start in your kitchen as this room generally has many hard flat surfaces. Use your signal and perform similar tasks to those outlined in the previous lessons.
5. Face your refrigerator and identify its shape. Move your head until you can sense the corner of it. You will notice that the response changes when your head passes the edge. At this point, you will be hearing the wall behind it.

6. With your eyes still closed and not depending on other things, move to another object like your cabinets. Try to distinguish the bottom edge.
7. Try crouching down to determine the level of the counter top.
8. Echolocate other objects without touching them and think to yourself, "the cupboard is 3 feet away from my face" or "the corner of the refrigerator is 10 inches from my nose."
9. Verify your accuracy. Once you have established where you think an object is, then and only then may you reach out to verify your estimate. If you are sighted or partially sighted, it's best to keep your eyes closed throughout the entire training session.

Are you getting the idea? What we're doing here is using prior knowledge of our environment as a framework or outline, verifying it using echolocation, and then re-verifying it with our hands. Gradually, you will be able to transition into more difficult environments – environments that are still familiar to you but have oddly shaped obstacles such as upholstered furniture or shelving. Become familiar with the sound and response of these environments and furnishings.

BEGINNER'S GUIDE TO ECHOLOCATION

Eventually, things will become clearer and you will become quicker at distinguishing shapes, sizes, distances and materials. Continually verify your estimates, but be cautious you are not reaching out to verify your estimate too soon. First, establish a clear estimate in your mind about what and where the object is. Then, reach your hand out only to where you think it should be, and if it is not there, continue echolocating instead of groping with your hand to find it.

WALKING A FAMILIAR PATH

1. Choose an environment you are familiar with. It should be a route that you often travel and is a fairly controlled environment, meaning that nothing is expected to change about it without notice. Pick a distance that is long enough to be challenging, but short enough that you will not get discouraged or lose track of where you are. Try somewhere between 20 and 100 yards. It might be good to have a few landmark obstacles as part of the path such as a car, a building, a fence, or a telephone pole. The larger objects will be easier to identify and it is a good place to start.
2. Setting your goal. Pick a landmark at the end of the path such as a telephone pole or a thick bush. Familiarize yourself with the lay of the land so that you will have a starting point and some familiarity. You'll most likely be attempting to navigate a path that you have previously used with a cane and you are familiar with the obstacles that you must avoid.
3. Visualizing your course. Once you know approximately where you're trying to get and what obstacles you need to avoid, it's time to set your course. Which side of the tree will you

walk on? Will the fire hydrant be to your left or to your right? Will you need to adjust your direction to navigate around obstacles? By doing this you will be able to break up your echolocation journey into smaller segments (i.e., after the fire hydrant, veer right to avoid the overhanging bush).
4. Echolocating. Beginning the echolocation journey, the first few steps you will be expecting. The immediate terrain and obstacles will be in your memory and you will easily navigate them without clicking. But, click anyway so that you can hear and get familiar with the echoes. As you approach your first large object, maybe a car, a tree, or a telephone pole, be aware that it is there. Listen for it and concentrate on the echoes. The goal here is not to touch anything that would give away the path, but if you are nervous about hitting your head, you can keep your hands up. However, keep them relatively low and out of the path of your clicks.
5. Objects that are closer to your starting point will be easier to pinpoint. Click in the direction that you are expecting to find an object. Once you have reached a landmark, acknowledge it, try to judge its distance, and then visualize your

path with respect to it. What is the next landmark? Is it the car on the left? Focus on the path and continue with a strong concentration and expectation of hearing the reverberation off the car. Once you get to it, acknowledge it. Notice the differences between the car and the telephone pole. The telephone pole, since it is round will sound the same from any direction. The car will change its reflective properties as your angle to it changes.

6. Reaching your goal. Once you have navigated yourself through you predetermined path, you should be at your end landmark. Be sure to stop when you have gotten to the landmark and acknowledge it. If possible, walk around the object still echolocating and clicking towards it. Try not to touch it! Are you sure this is the correct object, or is that thing you think is a telephone pole actually a bush? How far away from it are you?

7. Verify your success. Take out your cane or otherwise confirm the location. How close did you come to your goal? Keep clicking for a little bit to understand what you are hearing and correlate what you are hearing to what you know to be true. Were you hearing another echo from a nearby tree that threw you off? Did

you judge the distance accurately? In your head, go back through the path you just walked and try to judge how accurate you were when you estimated your distance to any other landmark objects.

USING THE VISUAL CORTEX TO BUILD NON-VISUAL IMAGERY

For blind or visually impaired people, it may be encouraging to know that there is evidence that the entire visual cortex of your brain is capable of being reallocated or rewired for use during echolocation. This part of your brain, being primarily unused, is capable of being allocated to anything relating to visual imagery, like dreams. It is also used for reading braille. (H. Burton, 2003.)

While I don't believe this is something you can actively practice during echolocation, after diligent training and commitment, it is possible to start recognizing objects through visualization. At a certain point in your training (and this point will of course be very different for each individual) the perception begins to change. Instead of having to think hard about a certain object at a certain distance, it is possible for the brain to actually register *images* instead of analytically interpreting sounds. This is called a non-visual image.

BEGINNER'S GUIDE TO ECHOLOCATION

PART 6

CONTINUING EDUCATION & PRACTICE

GETTING THE MOST OUT OF ECHOLOCATION

HOW CAN I BECOME AN EXPERT AT ECHOLOCATION?

The most well-known pioneer of teaching and spreading echolocation in today's world has started a foundation called *World Access for the Blind* (www.WorldAccessForTheBlind.org) and has made it his life's work to teach blind people to see using echolocation. His name is Daniel Kish, and he has developed methods of teaching blind mobility in ways that no one else has. I have spoken with Daniel and many of his colleagues at World Access for the Blind and can assure you that they will be able to help you get started learning how to become an expert echolocator. It is always suggested that for optimally effective training, one should study one-on-one with Daniel or one of the many instructors at World Access for the Blind. They provide a three-day intensive program that has been designed to make anyone a good active echolocation user in this short amount of time.

Other organizations around the world are beginning to implement the principles of active echolocation during their orientation and mobility training sessions. *Visibility* is an organization in Scotland (http://www.visibility.org.uk) which offers an echolocation training regimen to children ages 5 through 19 through their *BMobile Project.*

If you are sure that echolocation is for you, be sure to ask your local orientation and mobility specialist about the best way for you to learn.

Everyone learns differently and echolocation is not necessarily an easy skill to learn; everyone is born with the capacity for it, but implementation requires the right mindset. You must first have a good understanding of yourself, not just how you feel, interact with, and perceive the world, but the way you learn. Some people learn through hearing, some learn through touching, many people learn through teaching others, but regardless, for echolocation you need to keep an open mind and trust that you do in fact have the capacity to interpret the world in new and different ways. You may find that it's best to wait until inspiration strikes, or that certain moods help you open your mind and allow you to be fully engulfed in the learning process. Don't force it; it will come with time if you let it.

BEGINNER'S GUIDE TO ECHOLOCATION

"YOU GET OUT OF LIFE WHAT YOU PUT INTO IT."

ANONYMOUS

WHERE DO I GO FROM HERE?

Whether you choose to contact a mentor or train on your own to gain more confidence and understanding, I hope this book has provided the inspiration necessary to launch you into a successful practice of active echolocation. Like anything, if you want to learn it, you will. Still today, echolocation may not be considered a conventional method of approaching orientation and mobility. Don't ever let anyone tell you what you can't do or shouldn't do. There is only one person in the world who will truly ever know what you want to accomplish in life and that is YOU. If echolocation appeals to you, TRAIN! And, never stop training until you get exactly where you want to be. You get out of life what you put into it, so be diligent about your efforts, and don't let anyone or anything get in your way.

Echolocation will eventually become common practice for the visually impaired, but as of now, it needs your support. Share your knowledge with others and spread the word about the growing resources available for people curious about learning echolocation. It is a diligent step in increasing their independence or gaining a better understanding of the world around them.

BEGINNER'S GUIDE TO ECHOLOCATION

"TODAY I WILL DO WHAT OTHERS WON'T, SO TOMORROW I CAN ACCOMPLISH WHAT OTHERS CAN'T."

JERRY RICE

ABOUT THE AUTHOR

Tim Johnson is passionate about life and helping all people realize their dreams and accomplish their most aggressive goals. As a martial arts instructor, he works with young children as well as adults to help them understand their true potential and gain the confidence and ambition they need to grow into strong, independent people. He believes that no one should settle for anything less than remarkable and that life is a fantastic journey in which more is possible than we may ever know, but we should never stop trying to comprehend all that it has to offer. Our innate curiosity and motivation to improve ourselves is what makes us human and will always drive us to new heights.

As a full time engineer, Tim's approach to echolocation is an analytical, fact-based exploration of the subject. He encourages the understanding of fundamental concepts in order to gain a complete knowledge of a subject. Once the fundamental puzzle pieces are understood, we can then begin to piece them together to realize the bigger picture.

As a sighted person, he knows that his ability to echolocate might never equal that of a blind person who has used these skills every minute of the day for decades, and whose life literally depends on the amount of awareness he or she has. But, he has dedicated a great deal of time and effort to learning the concepts, intricacies, and applications of echolocation in his own life with a slightly different perspective in order to understand it to the best of his ability and share these lessons with those in need. His outside perspective aims to explore the intricacies of the beginner's learning process and has proven successful in relaying and articulating the basic concepts necessary for echolocation.

REFERENCES

ECHOLOCATION PROGRAMS

World Access for the Blind
(http://www.worldaccessfortheblind.org/)

BMobile Project from Visibility in the UK
(http://www.visibility.org.uk/)

INFORMATIONAL ARTICLES / WEBSITES

Getting Around by Sound: Human Echolocation
(http://blogs.plos.org/neuroanthropology/2011/06/14/getting-around-by-sound-human-echolocation/)

Behind the Curtain: Echolocation Woodstock
(http://behindthecurtain.us/2012/05/08/echolocation-woodstock/)

Environmental Graffiti – How Blind People Can Use Echolocation to See Like Bats
(http://www.environmentalgraffiti.com/news/news-how-blind-people-see-echolocation)

Echolocation – Reconditioning the Senses
(http://marcusbrillius.hubpages.com/hub/Echolocation-

Reconditioning-the-Senses-Could-this-help-rehabilitate-the-visually-impaired)

Visibility UK – Visual Impairment Training
(http://www.visibility.org.uk/what-we-do/training/)

Brian Bushway – Leading the Blind
(http://www.worldaccessfortheblind.org/sites/default/files/MBA90.91.pdf)

The Psychologist News - Echolocation
(http://www.thepsychologist.org.uk/blog/blogpost.cfm?catid=48&threadid=2083)

Learn Echolocation Blog (Author's Blog)
(http://learnecholocation.blogspot.com)

WHITE PAPERS

Echolocating Distance by Moving and Stationary Listeners
Lawrence D. Rosenblum, Michael S. Gordon, and Luis Jarquin
University of California, Riverside

Echolocation – What it is, How it Can Be Learned and Taught
Daniel Kish, M.A. and Hannah Bleier, M.A.

BEGINNER'S GUIDE TO ECHOLOCATION

Echolocation – How Can We Best Teach It?
Jim Blackshear
Stephen F. Austin State University

Directional Perception in the Human Auditory System
Susan J. Shaw
Journal of Undergraduate Sciences, Northwestern University

How Well Do We Know Our Own Conscious Experience? The Case of Human Echolocation
Eric Schwitzgebel, Michael S. Gordon
University of California

Blindness and Brain Plasticity: Contribution of Mental Imagery?
S. Lambert, E. Sampaio, Y. Mauss, C. Scheiber

Visual Imagery Without Visual Perception?
Helder Bertolo
Faculade de Medicina de Lisboa (Portugal)

Visual Cortex Activity in Early and Late Blind People
H. Burton
Department of Anatomy and Neurobiology, Washington University School of Medicine, St. Louis, Missouri
The Journal of Neuroscience, May 15, 2003